Primary
Science

PRIMARY SCIENCE

Knowledge and Understanding

Edited by Jenny Kennedy

London and New York

First published 1997
by Routledge
11 New Fetter Lane, London EC4P 4EE

Simultaneously published in the USA and Canada
by Routledge
29 West 35th Street, New York, NY 10001

Typeset in Plantin by M Rules

Printed and bound in Great Britain by
Redwood Books, Trowbridge, Wiltshire

British Library Cataloguing in Publication Data

A catalogue record for this book is available from the British Library

Library of Congress Cataloging in Publication Data

A catalogue record for this book has been requested

ISBN 0–415–12912–5

Contents

List of Figures   vii

Contributors   xi

Introduction   xiii

1 Life Processes
NIGEL SKINNER   1

2 Humans as Organisms
NIGEL SKINNER   9

3 Green Plants as Organisms
NIGEL SKINNER AND ANN GRAHAM   35

4 Variation and Classification
ANN GRAHAM AND NIGEL SKINNER   49

5 Living Things in Their Environment
ANN GRAHAM AND NIGEL SKINNER   59

6 Materials and Their Properties
GEOFFREY WICKHAM   79

7 Natural Materials: the Story of Rock
CARRIE BRANIGAN   95

8 Electricity
LINDA WEBB   105

9 Forces and Motion
JIM JARDINE AND JENNY KENNEDY   127

10 Light
JENNY KENNEDY   149

11 Sound
GEOFFREY WICKHAM   161

12 The Earth and Beyond
JIM JARDINE AND JENNY KENNEDY   173

Glossary   193

FIGURES

2.1	The human alimentary canal	16
2.2	A section through the human heart	25
2.3	The human respiratory system	27
2.4	The human skeleton	29
3.1	The structure of a typical flowering plant	38
3.2	The structure of a typical leaf	39
3.3	Generalised section through an animal-(insect-)pollinated flower	43
3.4	Generalised section through a wind-pollinated flower	43
3.5	Section through a broad bean seed	45
5.1	The carbon cycle	73
5.2	The nitrogen cycle	74
6.1	Investigating electrical conductivity	82
6.2	Particles in solids, liquids and gases	86
6.3	The water cycle	90
7.1	A sedimentary rock under a powerful hand lens, showing cemented grains (minerals)	98
7.2	An igneous rock under a powerful hand lens, showing the interlocking minerals	99
7.3	A metamorphic rock under a powerful hand lens, showing the minerals lined up	99
7.4	The rock cycle	103
8.1	Movement of an electron as it moves though a solid	108
8.2	Electron movement	108
8.3	An electrical circuit	110
8.4	A circuit to test for conducting and insulating materials	111
8.5	A resistor	114
8.6	Altering the resistance of a circuit	115
8.7	A potentiometer	116
8.8	An electric light bulb	117
8.9	A buzzer	117
8.10	An electric motor	118

8.11	Switches: (a) a simple switch (b) a push switch	119
8.12	International symbols for circuit components	119
8.13	Circuit diagrams	120
8.14	Series circuits	121
8.15	A parallel circuit	122
8.16	A parallel circuit with three bulbs	122
8.17	More complicated circuits	123
8.18	Circuit components	124
9.1	Forces which start things moving	129
9.2	Some forces on a bike which is being pushed along	130
9.3	A force is needed to change the movement of a bike	131
9.4	Forces can change the shape of an object	132
9.5	Forces in a tug-of-war	134
9.6	Balanced forces	135
9.7	A beach-ball in water	138
9.8	A beach-ball displaces water	139
9.9	Upthrust supports a beach ball	139
9.10	Paper falling	142
9.11	Investigating the force of (solid) friction	144
9.12	A balloon hovercraft	146
10.1	Shadows	154
10.2	Light scatters from a cat so it can be seen from all directions	155
10.3	The angles made by a ray of light before and after hitting a flat mirror	156
10.4	Some rays of light scattered from a spot on the face	157
10.5	How we see an image in a flat mirror	158
11.1	Pan pipes	163
11.2	Other ways to vibrate a column of air	164
11.3	A string telephone	165
11.4	Echo-sounding	165
11.5	Electric bell in a bell jar	166
11.6	Sound waves	167
11.7	Waves in a spring	167
11.8	Waves at high and low amplitudes	169
12.1	The sun's rays are very nearly parallel when they reach the earth	176
12.2	Many solid shapes can appear circular	177
12.3	Eclipses of the Sun by the Moon	177
12.4	Sun, Moon and Earth all lie in approximately the same plane	178
12.5	Changes in the Sun's apparent path throughout the year	180

12.6	The lengths of shadows in summer and in winter	182
12.7	(a) Plotting the path of the Sun across the sky	
	(b) Explanation of the apparatus	183
12.8	Different times of day and night	185
12.9	Side view of the tilted Earth in different positions as it orbits the Sun	186
12.10	The effects of the Earth's tilt on the Sun's altitude	187
12.11	Phases of the Moon	189
12.12	The Moon's twenty-eight phases	191

CONTRIBUTORS

Carrie Branigan BSc (Hons) Geology (University of Wales, Cardiff), taught 4–12-year-olds before becoming an Advisory Teacher. After four years as a lecturer at the University of Exeter, she is now an Inspector with Hampshire County Council and OFSTED.

Ann Graham BSc (Hons) Agricultural Microbiology (University of Nottingham), MSc in Dairying (University of Reading), has taught at the College of Technology, Belfast, and for the past twelve years has been a lecturer in the School of Education, University of Exeter. She is Chair of Governors at a primary school, where she also teaches occasionally.

Jim Jardine BSc (Hons) Physics (University of Edinburgh), MEd (Moray House College of Education), taught for many years in secondary schools in Scotland and at Moray House. He now assists with science and technology projects in primary schools. He has also taught and lectured extensively overseas and contributed through committee work to both the Association for Science Education and the Institute of Physics. He has received recognition of this work through several prizes for teaching – Fellowship of the Institute of Physics, the Bragg Medal and an OBE.

Jenny Kennedy BSc (Hons) Physics (University of London), MSc (University of Oxford), is a Lecturer in Education at the University of Exeter on both primary and secondary undergraduate programmes and secondary PGCE. She spent several years teaching in secondary comprehensive and direct-grant schools. Her research interest is in Initial Teacher Education, and she has held research posts at the University of Reading and the Schools Council. She is an external examiner for Cheltenham and Gloucester College of Higher Education.

Nigel Skinner BSc Zoology (University of London), PhD (Polytechnic of Central London), spent several years teaching in comprehensive and grammar schools in Wiltshire and is currently a junior-school governor and chair of the school's curriculum committee. His research interests include the teaching of science and biology at all levels.

Linda Webb BSc Physics (University of London), MSc (University of Oxford), works with both primary and secondary students at Homerton College, Cambridge, and previously taught in secondary comprehensive and grammar schools. Her research interests are children's learning and the use of IT in science.

Geoffrey Wickham BSc (Hons) Chemistry (University of Bristol), is Head of Chemistry at Queen Elizabeth's School, Bristol

JENNY KENNEDY

Introduction

Introduction

Jenny Kennedy

The main aim in writing this book has been to provide easily accessible science for primary school teachers and student teachers, particularly for those whose science background is limited. The book should also prove useful for teachers of science in the lower part of secondary schools and in middle schools. It should also be useful to science specialists who wish to revise their knowledge. We hope the book will help to build up teachers' scientific knowledge and to develop their understanding of the relevant science concepts. We are attempting to 'teach not tell', giving as far as is possible sound but informal explanations. Technical terms have been avoided where familiar words will do just as well. We hope the result is readable, understandable and informative. We have tried as far as possible to use exemplar material which we consider suitable for teachers' use in their teaching. We have also attempted to use vocabulary appropriate to the primary classroom.

As teachers improve their understanding of the science they are required to teach, stress in the classroom should lessen as confidence in the teaching of science grows. Both long-term schemes of work and short-term lesson plans should be easier to prepare. An appreciation of the development of science concepts should put teachers in a stronger position to plan for progression in their teaching and to select appropriately differentiated materials for different groups of pupils. As well as posing suitably targeted questions to pupils, teachers should find this book helpful in answering pupils' questions.

The members of the team of contributors have all taught extensively in schools and have contributed to initial teacher education and in-service courses. Each is a subject specialist in the areas on which they have written here. The book has been extensively trialled with ITE students and teachers on in-service courses, and revised accordingly. All subject content required by the current National Curriculum has been covered thoroughly. Sections within chapters are as far as possible free-standing, so teachers need only refer to relatively small segments as required. However, in many cases there would be advantages in studying more broadly. Where we have seen fit, additional material has been included: for example, the main chapter on materials (Chapter 6) is followed by 'Natural Materials: The Story of Rock'.

In order to enhance teachers' understanding, explanations are sometimes extended beyond those expected in the classroom. Within the chapters, the order in which the subject matter is presented is not necessarily that in which it appears within the National Curriculum document. We have tried to develop ideas in ways most appropriate to our purpose – facilitating the learning of adults: restructuring may be required for the classroom.

The style of writing in this book is basically didactic. However, we do not wish to imply that such a style is appropriate for the primary classroom. Furthermore, since this book tackles subject content, there is little reference to investigative or experimental science. It is inevitable that what is inherent in the text will, inadvertently, reveal something of the contributors' views of science. However, we do not tackle explicitly anything to do with the nature and process of science in the classroom. There is a danger that teachers will consider the teaching of subject knowledge and understanding, and of science investigation and experiment, as two distinct activities. This can be avoided by careful integration of practical work with subject content.

Pupils' own alternative views of the world mentioned within the text often survive intact even after very careful teaching. What is more, these ideas are often retained throughout childhood and into adult life. Research is under-way into teaching and learning strategies so that, having winkled out individual preconceptions, teachers should be better placed to encourage pupils to adopt, and to believe in, those ideas which the world scientific community generally accepts.

We have tried to raise teachers' awareness of these preconceptions by referring to them in the text. They could then be discussed in the classroom and evidence for them challenged. However, we are not yet in a position to make firm recommendations on how best to encourage pupils to discard or to adapt their misconceptions.

For further information in this area, readers are referred to reports from a national project, the SPACE project (see reference, page 124).

Bibliography

Driver, R. (1990–4) *Science Processes and Concept Exploration*, 8 vols. Liverpool: Liverpool University Press.

Kinder, K. and Harland, J. (1991) *The Impact of Inset: The Case of Primary Science*. London: National Foundation for Education Research.

Warren, P. (1988) *The Teaching of Physics*. London: Butterworth.

Wragg, E.C., Bennett, S.N. and Carré, C.G. (1989) 'Primary teachers and the National Curriculum'. *Research Papers in Education*, 4.3.

NIGEL SKINNER

1

Life Processes

Introduction   2

What is life?   2

The processes of life   3

Summary   6

1

LIFE PROCESSES

NIGEL SKINNER

INTRODUCTION

Living things share certain characteristics or 'life processes' which distinguish them from non-living things. To remain alive they must live in places that provide them with the things they need to keep their life processes going. Individual organisms will die, but life will go on (we hope!) because some will reproduce before they die. In this chapter the life processes common to animals and plants are discussed.

WHAT IS LIFE?

If children are asked the question 'How do you know that you are alive?' their responses will often include ideas about being able to walk and run, to make noises and talk, to think, to breathe, to see and hear, to think, and having a heart which beats. Some of these things are also exhibited by other living things but many are not. Clearly, plants do not walk or run and probably don't think much! Successful teaching about what it means to be alive needs to move pupils away from their 'human'-centred views towards a more general understanding of the concept of 'living'.

The things that we find around us can all be placed into one of three groups:

- those that are living;
- those that were living and are now dead;
- those that have never been living.

Familiar things belonging to each group are listed in the box:

Living	Once living	Never lived
All animals (including humans) and all plants	Wood and paper products Some fossil remains of plants and animals including coal and oil and products derived from them	Air, water, metals, salt, sugar and some rocks

It is not always easy to decide which group something is in. Difficulties arise because the characteristics which we use to recognise that something is alive are not always easy to detect (and are not displayed at all when something has died). Children sometimes think that if something moves or makes noises then it must be alive. Cars and mechanical toys, which clearly are not living, can do both. Plants, which are living, appear to do neither. Similarly, it is sometimes not easy to decide whether a living thing is still alive. Raw fruit and vegetables are still alive when they are eaten. Seeds may look completely lifeless but, when provided with appropriate conditions, may germinate and grow into new plants.

It is generally accepted that living things display, or have the capacity to display, certain characteristics which can be called 'processes of life'. This is what makes them different from things which never live.

THE PROCESSES OF LIFE

Some processes of life are more obvious and easy to understand than others. In explaining some of them it is difficult to avoid using the term 'cell'. Nearly all living things are made up of one or more distinct, very small units called cells. Consideration of the cellular organisation of living things will help more able, older children to understand the nature of all life processes.

Reproduction

The process which makes living things fundamentally different from non-living things is their ability to reproduce. There are two types of reproduction: sexual and asexual.

In sexual reproduction life begins in a new individual when two specialised types of cell (called gametes) join together. In animals the male gamete is a sperm cell and the female gamete an egg cell (see page 18). In flowering plants the male gametes develop inside pollen grains and the female gametes inside structures called ovules (see page 42). When male and female gametes join together a single-celled structure called a zygote is formed. The zygote will contain genetic material ('instructions') from both parents.

'Asexual' means 'without sex', and gametes are not involved in asexual reproduction. New individuals begin their existence by growing whilst attached to their (single) parent and then become separated and live independently. Familiar examples of this are provided by spider plants and the bulbs of daffodil plants. Some simple animals can reproduce asexually but humans and other vertebrates cannot.

Growth

Living things grow and develop, increasing in size and changing shape as they progress towards a mature body form. Growth in the tiny organisms consisting of a single cell results in that cell getting bigger. When it reaches a certain size the cell divides into two, each of which is smaller than the parent (i.e. the cell reproduces asexually). These cells grow until they are as big as the parent was and then they in turn divide. Growth in organisms whose bodies are made up of many cells requires repeated cell divisions. All humans begin life as a single cell. When fully grown we have millions of cells in our bodies.

All parts of an animal's body can grow, whereas growth in plants is restricted to specific regions such as the tips of shoots and roots. Plants also grow throughout their lives whereas animals have specific growth phases and usually stop growing once they attain a particular size. In humans this is at about 18–21 years of age but in most other animals it is at a much younger age. Although animals stop growing bigger some of their cells continue to divide. Cells which wear out quickly, for example skin cells and red blood cells, are continually being replaced. Some other types of cell, including muscle and nerve cells, cannot be replaced.

As organisms get bigger, structures develop to support them, for example the trunks and branches of trees and the skeletons of animals. The word 'skeleton' is most often used to refer to the bones found inside vertebrate animals. It is worth noting that invertebrate animals also have a skeleton. Some, like insects and crabs, have a hard outer covering which supports them. Soft-bodied invertebrates, like earthworms and jellyfish, are supported by the liquid or jelly-like material inside their bodies (see page 53).

Feeding

Living things need food for growth and energy. The food of humans and other animals comes from other living things. Animals eat food containing complex chemicals that need to be broken down into simpler ones by digestion before being reassembled into the chemicals their own bodies need (see page 14). In contrast, plants take in simple chemicals and turn these into the more complex chemicals they need. In green plants, the process of photosynthesis is very important – carbon dioxide and water are turned into sugars using energy from sunlight as 'fuel' (see page 40).

Movement

To obtain their food or to escape from danger, most animals need to be able to move around. This can involve swimming, wriggling, crawling, flying, hopping, walking or running. They use muscles to do this and, if the animal has a rigid skeleton, the muscles are attached to it. Some animals cannot move from one place to another, for example adult barnacles and mussels. These animals rely on food being brought to them by the water around them. Parts of plants are able to move, for example leaves and petals, but plants do not need to move around because the chemicals they need are all around them – in air, soil and water. Movement of plants is usually due to some cells dividing faster than others or to cells becoming bigger or smaller by taking in or losing water.

Sensitivity

Finding food, a mate and a suitable place to live requires animals to be sensitive to their surroundings and show appropriate behaviour patterns. Plants also need to respond to their environment; for example, they must make sure that their shoots grow upwards and their roots grow downwards. In animals it is the sensory part of the nervous system which detects change in the environment. The sensory cells are often gathered together in groups to form sense organs such as eyes or ears (see page 21). As well as these sense organs humans have sensory cells scattered throughout their skin and internal organs. These detect pressure, pain, heat and cold. The information collected is passed to the brain which controls how we react (behave) as a result of this knowledge. Any resultant change in behaviour involves our muscles (we might run away if we saw an angry bull), or our endocrine (hormone) system (we might stand our ground but start to sweat with fear).

Plants do not have nerve cells or a brain. They often produce minute amounts of chemicals which help them to respond to their environment. For example, if a plant is placed so that its shoot is bending away from the light a chemical collects on the lower side of the stem. The cells there divide more rapidly so that the shoot becomes upright and then bends towards the light.

Respiration

Energy is needed to keep all life processes going. It comes from a process called respiration which, in most cases, requires a supply of oxygen that is obtained by breathing. Oxygen is needed because during respiration food is slowly 'burned' to release the energy in it. When something burns, it is combined with oxygen.

Respiration occurs in all living cells and it is important to remember that plants as well as animals need to 'breathe'. Breathing is more obvious in animals because they need more energy than plants, for example when moving, and hence need to respire more quickly. Larger animals need to have a system for moving oxygen, food and other substances around the body to their cells; this is provided by their circulatory system.

Excretion

The processes which occur inside living cells result in useful products being made, for growth, repair and maintenance, for example. By-products which are not needed and which may be dangerous to the organism are also made. The removal of these is called excretion. Carbon dioxide and urea (a component of urine) are examples of by-products which are excreted by animals. Defecation is not an example of excretion. This is because the faecal material has never entered body cells. Faeces are undigested food material that remain inside the alimentary canal (the tube that carries food through the body) until they are got rid of by defecating.

SUMMARY

- Defining what is meant by life is not easy; one way of doing it is to identify those things which living things do that most non-living things are unable to do.

- Seven main 'characteristics of life' can be identified: the most important of these is reproduction.
- The others are growth, feeding, movement, sensitivity, respiration and excretion.

2

Humans as Organisms

NIGEL SKINNER

Introduction	10
The structure of the human body	11
Diet and role of the digestive system	11
Exercise and rest	13
Digestion	14
Reproduction, growth and development	18
Detecting and responding to change	21
The endocrine system	23
The circulatory system	24
Breathing: the respiratory system	26
Support and movement	28
The excretory system	30
Drug use and abuse	30
Summary	32

2

HUMANS AS ORGANISMS

NIGEL SKINNER

INTRODUCTION

The human species is just one of many millions of species that comprise the animal kingdom. In common with other animals, humans display the processes of life discussed in Chapter 1. In this chapter some of the basic concepts in human biology are discussed. The main emphasis is on how these are related to personal development and health.

Biologists use the terms 'organ' and 'organ system' when discussing the structure of living things, that is, how organisms are organised. An organ can be defined as a distinct structure which carries out a particular function within a living thing. Most people are happy to use the term 'organ' when talking about structures such as the heart and brain. It can also be used when discussing structures such as bones and muscles. Organs work in conjunction with others to form 'organ systems' that carry out their functions in a co-ordinated manner in the whole animal. For example, the heart and blood vessels together form the circulatory system.

The major organ systems and their functions are listed in the box.

Major organ systems	
Name of the system	*Function of the system*
Digestive	Feeding and digestion
Circulatory	Transport of materials around the body
Musculo-skeletal	Support and movement
Sensory and nervous	Detecting and responding to events
Endocrine	Production of hormones which influence many processes inside the body
Respiratory	Breathing and the release of energy from food
Excretory	Getting rid of waste products made in body cells
Reproductive	Producing offspring

This chapter discusses aspects of each of these and concludes with a short section on drug use and abuse.

THE STRUCTURE OF THE HUMAN BODY

An important unifying concept in biology is that the structures possessed by living things are closely related to their functions. When introducing the names of the different parts of the body to children the functions of these parts and the ways in which they are suited to them could be discussed. For example, young children could discuss walking and running in terms of the structure of their legs: these need to swing at the hip and to bend at the knees and ankles to get the feet in the right position. With older children, the structure and function of internal organs such as the heart and blood vessels could be considered. The heart is made of muscle because it has to keep beating. The blood vessels are long, pipe-shaped structures because they have to carry a liquid (blood) around the body. Approaching the study of their bodies in this way will introduce children to the names of many different parts of themselves, why they have these parts and why they are put together in the way that they are.

DIET AND THE ROLE OF THE DIGESTIVE SYSTEM

We are what we eat

The human body is made up of a number of different substances. The main types and amounts of each are listed in the box.

Main substances in the human body	
Substance	*Percentage in the body*
Water	65
Proteins	18
Fats	10
Carbohydrates	3
Mineral salts	3
Others, e.g. vitamins	1

Sources and functions of food

Food is needed for growth, energy and repair of damaged areas. A healthy or 'balanced' diet consists of the appropriate types of food in the correct quantities. There are six main classes of food. Their main sources and functions in the body are summarised in the box.

The main sources and function of the six classes of food		
Class of food	*Main source in our diet*	*Main functions in the body*
Proteins	Meat, fish, dairy produce, seeds and nuts	Growth and repair of body cells
Fats and oils	Fatty and oily foods, e.g. chips, crisps, cheese and cream	Energy source and store, insulation
Carbohydrates	Bread, potatoes, rice, pasta and sugar	Main source of energy
Minerals, e.g. iron and calcium	Depends on the mineral: iron is found in red meat; calcium in milk	Depends on the mineral: iron is needed for red blood cells; calcium for teeth and bones
Vitamins (there are many different types)	Depends on the type: many important ones are found in fresh fruit and vegetables	Prevention of 'vitamin-deficient' diseases
Fibre (roughage)	Unrefined cereals, fresh fruit and vegetables	Indigestible material which adds 'bulk' to food and helps prevent diseases of the alimentary canal

The amount of food needed by a person depends on their age, sex, body size and lifestyle. People who use a lot of energy in manual labour and exercise each day will need more food than those who lead an inactive life. Pregnant and breast-feeding women need extra food to be able to supply the needs of the growing baby.

An incorrect balance between the different food types can lead to malnutrition. A balanced diet is one in which the amount and variety of food eaten is enough, but not too much, to provide for all the needs of the body. If people eat more fat or sugar than they need they will become overweight because the excess will be stored in their bodies. Eating too much of these foods can also lead to tooth decay and diseases of the heart and arteries. People are more likely to eat too much fatty or sugary food because these taste particularly nice and are often available as snack foods such as crisps and chocolate bars.

Protein foods are generally more expensive and so are less likely to be eaten. If people are very poor they may be short of protein and this can mean that children do not grow properly and are not alert.

Eating fresh fruit and vegetables provides minerals and vitamins. People who do not eat enough vitamins will be generally unhealthy and more likely to suffer from infections. Some people take vitamin tablets, but this can be dangerous because some vitamins are poisonous if eaten in large amounts. Eating a variety of foods and not too much of any one provides a balanced diet which is essential for good health.

EXERCISE AND REST

Children do not usually need encouragement to be energetic. Most enjoy activities such as running around, cycling and other sports. Regular exercise benefits the body because it increases the efficiency of the respiratory and circulatory systems. It improves the ability to take in and use oxygen and the heart muscle becomes stronger and able to pump more blood with less effort. This makes the body more resistant to diseases which affect the heart, blood vessels and lungs. Other muscles also get stronger and the blood supply to bones improves so that they also become stronger.

Exercise uses energy which we get from the food we eat. If we eat more than our body needs the excess is stored as fat. Taking in only as much as we need is the most effective way of controlling body weight. Regular exercise can help because it uses up energy reserves which are stored as fat.

In contrast to being energetic, going to bed and sleeping is something which most children have to be persuaded to do. It is not entirely clear why we need to sleep but it is evidently essential for physical and mental well-being. During sleep, organs such as our lungs and heart have the minimum amount of work to do and brain cells are also rested. Different amounts of sleep are needed at different ages. New-born babies may sleep for 22 hours each day. At one year this reduces to about 14–15 hours. Five-year-olds need about 12½ hours, eleven-year-olds about 10½ hours and most adults about eight hours.

DIGESTION

Digestion is the term used to describe the process by which animals turn the relatively complex chemicals which they eat into the simpler ones which they can absorb. During digestion food is broken down both physically (into smaller pieces) and chemically (into simpler molecules). This process begins in the mouth and continues in a tube running through the body which is called the alimentary canal.

Digestion in the mouth

Before food is swallowed it is chewed. The teeth bite food and grind it up into smaller pieces. We have different types of teeth which perform different functions. These are described in the box.

Teeth

Tooth type	Shape	Function
Incisors	Sharp, chisel-shaped teeth which move past each other when we bite	Biting off pieces of food, for example when eating an apple
Canines	Similar to incisors but more pointed	Same as incisors
Molars and premolars	Cube-shaped teeth, with blunt tops called cusps, that meet when the jaws are closed	Grinding and crushing food into small pieces

Milk teeth and permanent teeth

Human babies are normally born with no teeth. By the age of one they usually have a set of milk teeth. In both upper and lower jaws there are four incisors, two canines and four premolars. These are replaced between the ages of 6 and 12 by a set of permanent teeth with four or six molars in addition to the other types listed above.

The part of a tooth which protrudes into the mouth is called the crown. It is covered with the hardest material found in the body – enamel. This is a non-living substance made mainly of calcium salts. The enamel covers the living part of teeth which has nerves and blood vessels running through it.

Care of teeth

'Permanent' teeth are not always permanent! They can be lost through injury or, more commonly, as a result of tooth decay or gum disease.

Tooth decay occurs when holes (cavities) form in the tooth enamel. These are caused when bacteria which live on the surface of the teeth release an acid that can dissolve enamel. Bacterial growth in the mouth is promoted by the presence of sugars. The best way to prevent tooth decay is to avoid sweets and sugary drinks. Toothpaste and drinking water that contains small quantities of fluoride can strengthen enamel and also help prevent tooth decay.

Gum disease occurs when bacteria get into the spaces between the gums and the enamel surface of the teeth. This can result in the destruction of fibres which fix the teeth to the jaw bone. The teeth then become loose and may fall out. The best way to prevent this is by regular brushing to remove the layer of plaque which contains the potentially harmful bacteria.

Digestion in other parts of the alimentary canal

The main functions of the organs that form the alimentary canal are summarised in the box and their arrangement in the body is shown diagrammatically in Figure 2.1. The liver is an organ which does not form part of the alimentary canal but is connected to it. It is the largest organ inside the body and may weigh up to 2 kg in adults. It has at least 500 functions. One of these is to receive and begin to process the food absorbed into the blood by the small intestine.

Figure 2.1

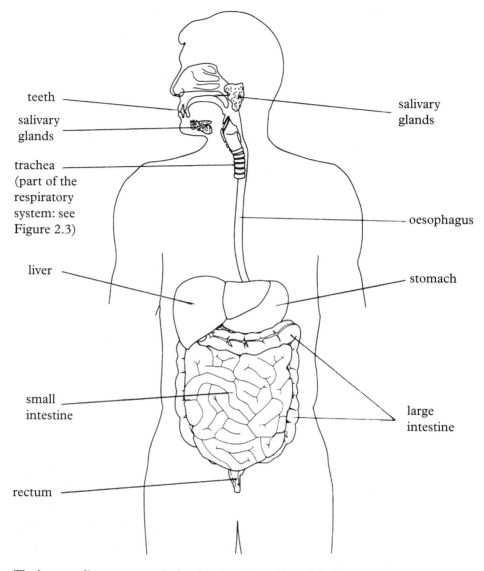

teeth

salivary glands

salivary glands

trachea (part of the respiratory system: see Figure 2.3)

oesophagus

liver

stomach

small intestine

large intestine

rectum

The human alimentary canal, also showing the position of the liver

The alimentary canal

Organ	Structure	Main functions
Oesophagus	Muscular tube	Pushes food from the mouth to the stomach
Stomach	Muscular 'bag'	Physical breakdown of food to a soup-like consistency. Chemical breakdown of some food types
Small intestine	Long (about 7 m in adults), thin-walled tube with a small (about 3 cm) diameter. The wall has many folds to increase the surface area through which absorption can take place	Digestion is completed and digested food is absorbed
Large intestine	Tube about 2 m long and 6 cm in diameter	Absorption of water
Rectum	Short (20 cm), muscular tube	Storage of indigestible food. Pushes out the faeces during defecation

Chemical digestion

The chemical breakdown of food in our alimentary canal is made possible by chemicals called digestive enzymes. Enzymes are chemicals in the body which speed up chemical reactions. Some, such as the digestive enzymes, are involved in speeding up the breakdown of large chemical molecules into smaller ones. They are needed because most of the food that we eat is made up of molecules that are too big to pass from our alimentary canal into our blood. Other enzymes are involved in speeding up reactions inside cells which change the small molecules which are absorbed into larger molecules that the body needs.

Any one type of enzyme acts on only one particular type of food substance, so we produce different enzymes to break down fats, carbohydrates and proteins. The digestive enzymes are produced by our bodies in glands called exocrine glands which empty into the upper part of the alimentary canal, or in special cells in the lining of the alimentary canal. When the breakdown of food is complete (we call it digestion) the simple food molecules are absorbed into the blood from the small intestine. There is always some food which cannot be digested. This is called fibre and is needed to help push food through our alimentary canals. Most of the water mixed with the food is absorbed from the large intestine.

REPRODUCTION, GROWTH AND DEVELOPMENT

Producing offspring

Reproduction in humans requires two different types of cell to join together. Sperm cells from males must fertilise egg cells from females. The obvious differences between the male and female reproductive systems are due to the different functions they perform.

The male system has two main functions:

● to produce large numbers of sperm cells;
● to pass these cells into the female reproductive system.

To carry out these functions it has three main organs: the testes (singular: testis); the sperm duct (or sperm tube); and the penis. Sperm cells are made in the two testes. These are found outside the main body cavity in a bag-like structure called the scrotum. Sperm cells leave the body via the sperm ducts which join another tube called the urethra. This runs through the middle of the penis. The urethra also carries urine out of the body (but not at the same time as sperm cells!).

The functions of the female reproductive system are:

● to produce egg cells;
● to maintain and nourish the developing offspring before they are born.

Eggs are produced in the ovaries. Human females have two ovaries. A tube called the oviduct (egg-tube or fallopian tube) leads from each ovary to the uterus (womb). From here another tube called the vagina leads to the body surface. Unlike the situation in males, a separate tube carries urine out of the body.

Bringing eggs and sperm together: sexual intercourse In humans and all other mammals the fertilisation of egg cells occurs inside the female body. Sperm cells are passed into the female during sexual intercourse. Before intercourse a male's penis becomes erect as spaces inside it become filled with blood. It is similar to what happens when a rubber balloon is blown up. As more air (blood) goes in, the balloon (penis) changes from being a small, floppy structure into a larger, hard structure. The erect penis is put inside the vagina of the female. Rhythmic movement of the penis in the vagina results in semen, a white liquid containing sperm cells, being pumped out of the testes into the vagina. This is called ejaculation. Sperm cells have a long 'tail' and swim by beating this behind them. They swim through the uterus into the oviducts. If there is an egg in one of the oviducts one of the sperm cells may fertilise it.

Fertilised eggs travel down the oviduct and develop into a ball of cells called an embryo. When this reaches the uterus it becomes embedded in the soft uterus wall and grows into a structure called a foetus – a miniature human being.

Growth and the main stages in the human life-cycle

Growth obviously involves an increase in size. Development is the term used for the changes which take place as growth occurs. Growth without development would result in 'grown-ups' looking very strange and behaving very oddly. As we grow, changes occur in our body proportions, our diet, our powers of movement, our ability to sense what is happening around us and our patterns of behaviour.

Body proportions Changes in body proportions occur because at different times different parts of the body grow at different rates. During foetal development the head grows quickly. Following birth the head grows relatively slowly. By the age of four the brain is almost fully grown. In contrast, the reproductive organs grow very slowly to begin with. Their maximum rate of growth occurs during adolescence.

Diet As people grow, their food requirements change. Babies are fed on milk until they are able to digest more solid food. During rapid periods of growth, such as early childhood and adolescence, proportionally more food is required. Some of the other changes which occur as people grow are summarised in the box.

The main stages in human development

Stage in development	Approximate age range (years)	Main characteristics and developments
Baby	0–1	Completely dependent on adults, limited movements and behaviour patterns
Toddler	1–2.5	Still dependent on adults, learning to walk, talk and feed themselves
Nursery child	2.5–5	Gradually becoming more independent, learning to dress themselves and to socialise. Early ideas about numbers and letters
Junior child	5–11	'Formal' schooling – development of reading, writing, numeracy, oracy and practical skills. Learning about the outside world in a 'theoretical' as well as 'practical' way
Adolescence	11–18	Formal schooling/training continues. Rapid growth and development of sexual maturity takes place during puberty. Becoming increasingly independent of adults
Adulthood	18+	Adult life: responsibilities to society, own children and parents
Old age	65+	Problems associated with ageing – loss of mobility and 'faculties'. May become dependent on others again

Becoming sexually mature The period of life between being a child and becoming an adult is called adolescence. Biologically this extends from about the age of 10 to the age of 19. Puberty is the name given to the time during adolescence when the reproductive organs become mature. The age at which puberty occurs varies from person to person. In girls it usually starts at about 11 years, in boys at about 12 years. The changes which take place during adolescence and puberty are described in the box.

**A summary of the main changes which take place
during adolescence and puberty**

Boys	*Girls*
Sex organs (penis and testes) get larger. Testes begin to make sperm cells	Ovaries start to release eggs. Menstruation (periods) starts
Hair begins to grow in the pubic region, on the face, chest and under the arms	Pubic and underarm hair begins to grow
Shoulders get broader	Hips get wider, breasts enlarge and more body fat grows on the hips and thighs
Voice deepens and behaviour changes	Behaviour changes

DETECTING AND RESPONDING TO CHANGE

To detect changes, both around us and inside us, we have a variety of senses. To respond to these changes in an appropriate way we need to have a system which processes the information received by the sense organs and sends messages to muscles or other 'effector' organs. This is the role of the nervous system. It has two main parts: the central nervous system and the peripheral nervous system. The central nervous system consists of the brain and the spinal cord. It is important that this does not get damaged, and it is protected by the bones of the skull and the vertebral column ('backbone'). The peripheral nervous system comprises all the nerve fibres which lead to and from the brain and spinal cord.

Human senses

It is often said that humans have just five senses: sight, hearing, smell, taste and touch. In fact, the human sensory system can respond to many more things. It also receives information from inside the body as well as from the outside world. For example, we know when we need food because we feel hungry. The box illustrates some of the diversity of the sensory system.

Some human senses

Name of the sense	Part of the body which detects the information	Form the information takes	'Usefulness' of the sense
Sight or vision	Eyes	Colour, movement, shape of things, etc.	Guides movement, e.g. towards food, away from danger
Hearing	Ears	Sounds	Communication by speech
Balance	Ears	Movements of the head	Keeping body upright
Position sense	Receptors in muscles	Whether muscles are contracted or relaxed	Co-ordinating body movements
Hunger	Receptors in stomach wall	Stretching of the stomach wall	Whether food is needed
Smell	Nose	Different smells associated with different things	Fresh food smells 'good', decaying food smells 'off'
Taste	Tongue	Responses to sweet, sour, salty and bitter tastes	Taste and smell of food give the sensation of flavour
Touch	Skin	'Feel' of things	Controlling the way we touch and move objects
Temperature	Skin and internal organs	How hot or cold something is	Preventing burns. Helping to keep the body temperature constant
Pain	Skin and internal organs	Unpleasant sensations	Learn from experience that certain things can cause physical pain, e.g. knives. Alerts us to damage, e.g. broken arm, or disease, e.g. 'tummy ache'

The nervous system

The information received by the sensory system is converted into 'messages' which can be sent around the body in the nervous system. The central nervous system processes the information it receives from the sensory cells and organs and co-ordinates the appropriate responses. If movement is required, messages will be sent to muscles. For example, when a hungry person sees a ripe-looking apple on a tree the following sequence of events might occur:

- the eyes send a message to the brain that what seems to be some suitable food is available;
- the brain processes this information and decides that it would be a good idea to eat it;
- messages are sent to the muscles in the arm and hand and the apple is picked;
- touch and temperature receptors in the hand collect more information about the apple. If it is soft (possibly rotten) or too hot or cold (unlikely!) the brain may decide that it is not a good idea to eat it;
- if it is to be eaten, messages are sent to bring the apple towards the mouth;
- receptors in the nose may now send messages to the brain. If the apple smells unpleasant, the person may decide not to eat it;
- if the apple smells nice, messages are sent that say 'bite it';
- taste receptors in the tongue now send messages about the taste of the apple: if it tastes good, eating will continue;
- if the ears receive information along the lines of 'Who said you could eat my apple?' in a loud aggressive voice, eating may quickly stop!

THE ENDOCRINE SYSTEM

The nervous system is involved in co-ordinating responses that need to occur quickly. The endocrine system co-ordinates responses that usually need to occur over a longer period of time. Processes such as growth, development of reproductive organs and digestion are all influenced by hormones. The endocrine system is made up of a number of structures called glands. These produce chemicals called hormones or 'chemical messengers'. They are released directly into the blood but only affect the particular cells with which they can interact. These are called the target cells of the hormone. For example, growth hormone, which is produced by the pituitary gland in the brain, acts on the cells of the skeleton and its attached muscles to increase their rate of growth and to maintain their size. A few children who do not have enough of this hormone are given daily injections of it to help them to grow to normal size. Another hormone which is sometimes in short supply is insulin. This is produced by certain cells in the pancreas. It acts to decrease the levels of sugar in the blood by encouraging body cells to take it in and use it or store it. People who do not produce enough insulin are said to have diabetes. They have to eat a diet which is very low in sugar and may need injections of insulin as well.

A hormone which has a relatively rapid effect on the body is adrenalin, sometimes called the 'fight or flight' hormone. It is produced by the adrenal glands when a person is alarmed or frightened by something and it is responsible for the familiar feeling of having 'butterflies in your tummy'. It helps to prepare the body for the extra effort and energy demands that may be involved in either running away from or standing up to danger. It does this by, amongst other things, increasing the heart, breathing and respiration rates.

THE CIRCULATORY SYSTEM

All the living parts of an animal's body need to receive oxygen, water and nutrients. Waste products such as carbon dioxide also need to be taken away. In mammals these materials are transported through the body in the bloodstream. Blood flows through tubes called blood vessels. Together with the heart, these form the circulatory system.

The structure of the heart

The heart is a muscular organ which pumps blood through the blood vessels. The human heart is about the size of an adult fist and is made up of four chambers as shown diagramatically in figure 2.2.

The structure of blood vessels

There are three main types of blood vessel in the circulatory system: arteries, veins and capillaries. Arteries carry blood away from the heart to the capillaries. They have relatively thick, muscular walls to withstand the high

Figure 2.2

 deoxygenated blood

 oxygenated blood

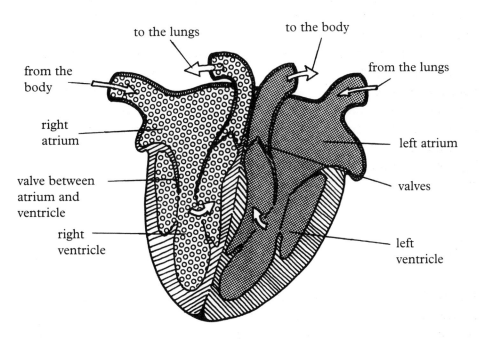

A section through a human heart, with associated blood vessels
Note: Arrows show the direction of blood flow

pressure of the blood that passes through them. Capillaries are microscopically small vessels with very thin walls. Materials such as oxygen, carbon dioxide and dissolved nutrients can pass across their walls, in and out of the surrounding body cells. Capillaries join with other capillaries and form veins which carry blood back to the heart. When it comes out of the capillaries blood is at a much lower pressure than when it enters them. This means that veins do not need to have such muscular walls as arteries and that they also need to have valves in them to prevent blood flowing backwards (see below).

Circulation and the pumping action of the heart

As the term circulation suggests, blood flows in a 'circuit', always returning to the heart (which pumps it around again) and the lungs (where it collects oxygen and loses carbon dioxide). Blood also absorbs nutrients from the small intestine as it circulates. The chambers of the heart (atria and ventricles) pump blood by rapidly contracting and squeezing the blood out. The two atria are much less muscular than the two ventricles. This is because their function is to receive blood and then pump it the short distance to the ventricles which lie immediately below them. Blood that is returning to the heart from all parts of the body except the lungs enters the right atrium which pumps it to the right ventricle. This pumps it to the lungs to pick up oxygen and get rid of carbon dioxide. It returns to the heart where it is received by the left atrium which pumps it to the left ventricle. This then pumps it to all the other parts of the body. The left ventricle has to pump blood further than any of the other chambers and is the most muscular part of the heart.

Valves To prevent blood flowing in the wrong direction a system of valves is needed. There are heart valves between the right atrium and the right ventricle, between the left atrium and the left ventricle and at the base of the main arteries that carry blood away from the heart (see figure 2.2). Valves are also present in veins (see above).

The effect of exercise on circulation When a person is asleep or very relaxed, little energy is needed to keep their life processes going. When they are exercising, much more energy is needed. The extra energy comes from an increase in the rate of respiration inside body cells (see page 28). Cells need more oxygen and nutrients for this. To supply these, the heart beats more quickly, causing blood to circulate more quickly. This can be detected easily because the faster beating of the heart causes a corresponding rise in the pulse rate. This occurs because the pulse is a direct response to the pumping action of the heart. The increase in pressure that occurs each time the heart beats causes a surge of blood through the arteries which can be felt as a pulse in those arteries which lie close to the body surface, for example at the wrist and neck.

BREATHING: THE RESPIRATORY SYSTEM

All mammals breathe air which enters and leaves their bodies through the nose or mouth. It passes through a tube called the windpipe or trachea which we can feel at the front of our necks. Inside the rib cage the windpipe divides into two branches called bronchi (singular: 'bronchus') which go to the lungs. This is shown diagrammatically in figure 2.3.

Figure 2.3

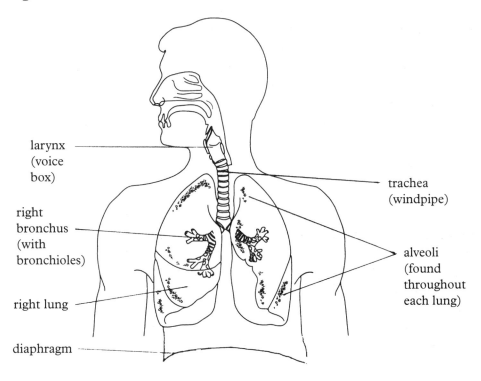

The human respiratory system

The lungs are often thought to be balloon-like structures but they are actually more like sponges. The tubes in the lungs branch repeatedly and end in microscopically small air spaces called alveoli (singular: 'alveolus'). A fully grown human will have about 150 million alveoli in each lung, which provides a total surface area of about 90 square metres. This is needed to provide a large, thin surface through which the gases oxygen and carbon dioxide can pass. Each tiny alveolus is surrounded by blood capillaries, and oxygen passes from the air into the blood and carbon dioxide (a by-product of respiration, see page 28) passes from the blood into the air.

Ventilation of the lungs

Breathing in and out is called ventilation. It results from a sequence of movements which alternately increase and decrease the volume of the space inside the rib cage. Two sets of muscles contract to increase this volume and draw air into the lungs:

- the diaphragm (a muscular sheet across the bottom of the rib cage) contracts and moves downwards;
- muscles connecting ribs together contract and raise the rib cage upwards and outwards.

The lungs are slightly elastic and air is pushed out of them as they get smaller when the muscles of the rib cage and diaphragm relax.

Respiration inside body cells

Blood carries oxygen to all the living cells inside the body which use it to release energy from food, as discussed in Chapter 1. When exercising, more energy is needed. This requires more oxygen and produces more carbon dioxide. To supply the extra oxygen and take away the potentially harmful carbon dioxide, both the ventilation rate and heart rate increase during exercise.

SUPPORT AND MOVEMENT

The musculo-skeletal system

Muscles and the skeleton form the musculo-skeletal system. To appreciate the importance of this system consider what would happen if it were not there:

- taking away the bones would result in the body collapsing into a relatively formless 'blob';
- this 'blob' would find it difficult to move since the muscles inside it would have no rigid bones to pull against when they contract;
- the 'blob' would also be very vulnerable since delicate internal structures such as the brain, spinal cord, heart and lungs would have no hard protective covering.

Figure 2.4

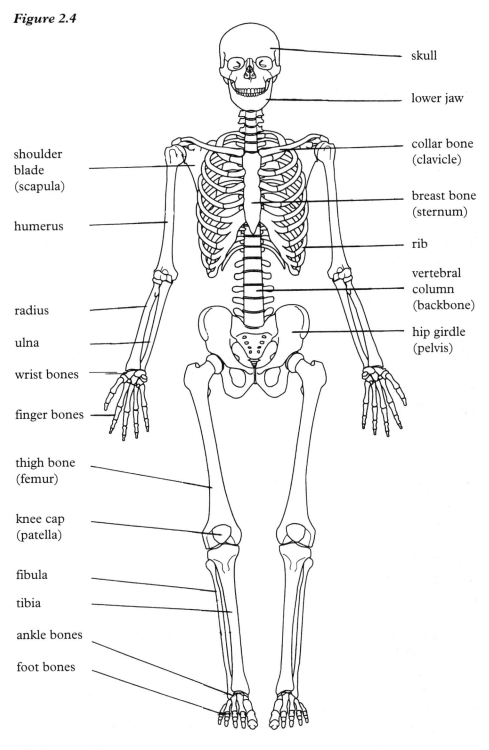

skull

lower jaw

collar bone
(clavicle)

shoulder
blade
(scapula)

breast bone
(sternum)

humerus

rib

vertebral
column
(backbone)

radius

hip girdle
(pelvis)

ulna

wrist bones

finger bones

thigh bone
(femur)

knee cap
(patella)

fibula

tibia

ankle bones

foot bones

The human skeleton

Thus, the skeleton has three main functions:

- to support the body;
- to provide attachment points for muscles, allowing movement to occur;
- to protect soft internal parts of the body: the skull protects the brain, the vertebral column protects the spinal cord, and the rib cage protects the lungs and heart.

The human skeleton

Mammals have an internal skeleton consisting of bones held together by muscles. The main bones of the human skeleton are shown in figure 2.4. The biological names for some of these bones are used where there is no easier alternative. 'Vertebral column' is a better term than 'backbone' because this 'bone' is actually made up of many small bones which fit together to form a column.

THE EXCRETORY SYSTEM

The two main excretory products of humans are carbon dioxide and urea. Carbon dioxide is formed as a by-product of respiration and is excreted by the lungs (see page 27). Urea is formed from excess proteins and is made in the liver. It passes into the bloodstream and then to the kidneys. Humans have two kidneys which lie one each side of the vertebral column just below the rib cage at the back of the body. They have two main functions:

- to filter waste products such as urea out of the blood;
- to maintain the correct amount of water in the body.

Waste products and excess water are passed from the kidney to the bladder. This stores them before they are passed out of the body as urine.

DRUG USE AND ABUSE

Substances other than food which are taken into the body and affect it in some way are called drugs. The same substance may have beneficial or detrimental effects depending on why it is taken and how much is taken. Drugs have benefited people in many ways, for example through relieving pain and helping to cure or alleviate the effects of diseases. Their misuse can result in increasing the chances of getting various diseases and may lead to early death.

Medicines

Nearly all children will have been given medicine, either bought over the counter or prescribed by a general practitioner, before they are very old. They will have experience of taking the correct dose and the notion that medicines help to 'make you better'.

The drugs most often bought in shops are pain-relieving (analgesic) drugs based on aspirin or paracetamol. The type of drug most commonly prescribed to a child is an antibiotic. Unlike analgesics, which relieve the symptoms of an illness, antibiotics kill bacteria, thereby removing the cause. Many common childhood illnesses such as coughs and colds are caused by viruses. Antibiotics have no effect on viruses. However, a viral infection may reduce the body's natural defences against bacteria (see page 71) and lead to a bacterial infection. If this occurs, an antibiotic may be prescribed.

Harmful drugs

Tobacco, alcohol and other drugs are substances which have effects on the body which, although they may be pleasurable, can lead to the normal life processes becoming disrupted and to a variety of harmful effects.

The harmful effects of tobacco

Respiratory diseases The lungs and the tubes leading to them produce a sticky liquid called mucus that traps dirt and microbes. On the surface of the cells lining the air tubes and lungs of a healthy respiratory system there are microscopically small hairs called cilia which beat to and fro and remove this mucus. Tobacco smoke damages cilia and as a result mucus begins to build up in the lungs. A 'smoker's cough' may develop which expels the mucus but, in doing so, damages the surface of the lungs. This results in a disease called emphysema in which breathing is painful and difficult. The build-up of mucus in the bronchi also leads to an increased risk of bronchitis.

Cancer A number of substances in tobacco smoke are carcinogenic (cancer-inducing). A cancer occurs when body cells divide in an uncontrolled way, resulting in the growth of a tumour. Smokers are far more likely than non-smokers to develop mouth, throat and lung cancer.

Heart disease Smoking increases both the tendency of blood to clot and the rate at which fatty material is deposited in the arteries. Coronary heart disease occurs when the arteries which supply the heart muscles (the coronary arteries) become narrow. If they are blocked by a clot then heart failure (a 'heart attack') occurs. High blood pressure, excessive animal fat in the diet and lack of exercise are other factors which can increase the risk of coronary heart disease.

Health risks associated with alcohol Alcohol has its effects by reducing the efficiency of the 'message-sending' and co-ordinating role of the central nervous system. This reduces inhibitions and, in small quantities, relieves anxiety. It also impairs judgement and reduces the ability to carry out activities that require co-ordination and skill, such as driving. Accidents, especially road accidents, are a major health hazard associated with alcohol. Alcohol in the body is broken down by the liver. Excessive amounts of alcohol can kill liver cells and result in liver cirrhosis which can lead to premature death.

Other harmful drugs There are obviously many other drugs which can be harmful if misused. Using any drug over a long period of time can result in people becoming tolerant of the drug and needing more of it to achieve the desired effect. This can lead to complete dependence on the drug and to all the problems associated with drug addiction.

SUMMARY

- Humans are members of the animal kingdom.
- All humans begin their life as a single cell.
- Adults have a body made up of millions of cells.
- These are grouped into organs which work together as organ systems. The main organ systems and their functions are:
  (a) the digestive system, which processes food inside the body;
  (b) the circulatory system, which transports materials around the body;
  (c) the muscles and skeleton, which support and move the body;

(d) the sensory and nervous systems, which detect changes and co-ordinate any immediate responses which may be needed;

(e) the endocrine system, which co-ordinates longer-lasting processes such as growth and development;

(f) the respiratory system, which is concerned with breathing (or 'ventilation') and energy production inside body cells;

(g) the excretory system, which gets rid of unwanted by-products of the chemical reactions inside cells;

(h) reproductive systems, which make gametes and, in the female, sustain and nourish the developing foetus.

- A healthy lifestyle requires a balanced diet, exercise and sufficient rest.
- Using drugs appropriately can help to maintain good health. Misuse of drugs can lead to physical illnesses and mental disorders.

NIGEL SKINNER AND ANN
GRAHAM

3

Green Plants as Organisms

Introduction   36

The structure and function of flowering
    plants   37

Nutrition and growth of flowering plants   40

Reproduction of flowering plants   42

The life-cycle of flowering plants   46

Summary   46

3

GREEN PLANTS AS ORGANISMS

NIGEL SKINNER

ANN GRAHAM

INTRODUCTION

Plants are organisms made up of many cells that make their own food by photosynthesis. Most plants are mainly green in colour because they contain the green pigment called chlorophyll which is essential for photosynthesis. Plants which do not have green leaves, for example copper beech trees, do possess chlorophyll but other pigments mask its green colour (see page 40).

The most successful and abundant land plants are those which reproduce by making seeds. There are two main groups of seed-bearing plant. One group produces seeds which are not enclosed inside fruits. The most familiar members of this group are coniferous (cone-bearing) trees like the Scots pine. The other group produces seeds inside fruits. These are the flowering plants. There are about 300,000 different species of flowering plant, more than all other types of plant put together. Most live on land but some live in fresh water and a few types are able to live in sea water. Some are relatively small, for example daisies and buttercups. Some, like horse chestnut trees, are very large. Intermediate in size are plants such as roses and rhododendrons that we call shrubs. Trees and shrubs have stems and side-stems (usually called trunks and branches) which contain wood – we call them 'woody' plants. Flowering plants that do not have wood in them are called 'herbaceous' plants or 'herbs'. (This is a different use of the word from the culinary term 'herb'.)

The named examples of flowering plants referred to above produce structures that most people would be happy to call flowers (although flowers on trees are more commonly called 'blossom'). Their flowers are colourful, easy to see and are often scented. It comes as a surprise to some people to find out that grasses are also flowering plants. This is because grass flowers are not colourful, scented or very obvious. Many kinds of tree also produce inconspicuous flowers or structures which, although they are flowers, are often called something else, for example, hazel catkins and 'pussy willow'. Differences between flowers occur because they are adapted to different methods of pollination.

This chapter considers the following aspects of flowering plants:

- their structure and function;
- their nutrition and patterns of growth;
- their reproduction;
- their life-cycles.

THE STRUCTURE AND FUNCTION OF FLOWERING PLANTS

Figure 3.1 is a diagram illustrating the main parts of a flowering plant. Four main 'organ systems' can be distinguished: roots, stems and side-stems, flowers and leaves. The structure and functions of roots, stems and side-stems are discussed below. Leaves and flowers are discussed in the sections on plant nutrition and reproduction which follow this section.

Roots: organs of anchorage and absorption

There are two main types of root system in flowering plants. Many species have a main root with side roots branching off it, e.g. trees, dandelions and other 'broad-leaved' species. Grasses and other 'narrow-leaved' species, such as onions, do not have a main root. Instead, they have a number of fibrous roots which grow out from the base of the stem.

Anchorage As anyone who has ever tried to dig up a tree or pull up a dandelion or grass plant will know, root systems are very good at anchoring plants firmly in the soil. Being fixed in place prevents animals pulling up plants when they are eating them. The extensive root system of trees enables them to stand upright and prevents them being blown over by strong winds.

Absorption Roots are vital for absorbing water and other chemicals that plants need from the soil around them. To help them do this, many tiny hairs called 'root hairs' grow out into the soil near the tips of each root. These increase the surface area over which absorption can occur.

Figure 3.1

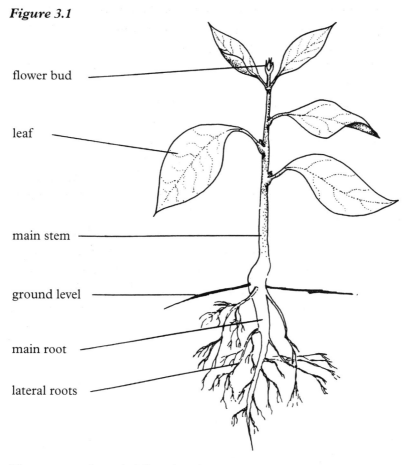

flower bud

leaf

main stem

ground level

main root

lateral roots

The structure of a typical flowering plant

Stems and side-stems: organs of support and transport

Support Flowering plants need to stand upright for three main reasons:

- to get their leaves into a good position for absorbing light;
- to hold their flowers up where they are more likely to be pollinated by insects or the wind;
- to disperse their seeds more widely and thus be able to colonise new areas by increasing the efficiency of wind or animal seed dispersal.

Trees and shrubs have large amounts of wood in their stems and side-stems. We usually refer to these structures as trunks and branches. Having this rigid support material enables them to grow much taller than non-woody plants. This is very important in woodlands and forests where plants will be competing with each other for space and light (see page 63).

Non-woody plants (herbs) do not have a solid supporting framework. They can only stand upright when there is plenty of water in their cells. If they do not have enough, the cells shrink and the plant wilts.

Transport Stems and trunks enable flowering plants to stand upright. As they grow taller the distance between the roots and the leaves will obviously increase. Water and mineral salts are absorbed through the root system and food is made in the leaves. A transport system is therefore needed to move substances between the roots and leaves.

Most water and mineral salts move through pipe-shaped cells which have no living contents. These cells are found in all parts of a plant. They have thicker walls than other types of cell and play an important role in supporting the plant. Most of the wood found in roots, trunks and branches is made of this type of cell. These cells also help provide a 'skeleton' for leaves (see figure 3.2).

Figure 3.2

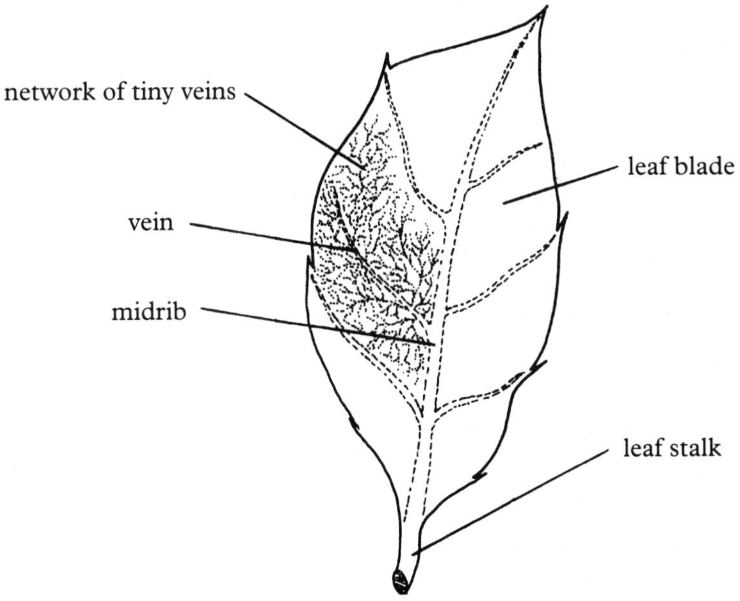

The structure of a typical leaf

Dissolved food substances are carried in elongated living cells running through plants. In woody plants these cells are found in the inner bark. If a ring of bark is cut right round a tree food cannot get down to the roots. The root system dies because it gets no food and eventually the whole tree will die.

NUTRITION AND GROWTH OF FLOWERING PLANTS

Photosynthesis

Photosynthesis is the term used for the process which green plants use to make food; when animals eat plants, it becomes their food too. Plants make their food from carbon dioxide and water, using energy from sunlight. Initially a type of sugar is made. This sugar can be used by the plant as a source of energy or as a raw material to help make the other types of chemicals that the plant needs, such as starch for storage in, for example, potato tubers. Many of these other chemicals require additional substances which the plant absorbs as mineral salts from the soil.

The word 'photosynthesis' comes from two other words: 'photo' meaning something to do with light (as in the word 'photograph') and 'synthesise' which means making something by combining other things together. In photosynthesis light energy is used to combine carbon dioxide and water. Light is absorbed by pigments (coloured substances) which are found in those parts of a plant where photosynthesis occurs. Most photosynthesis occurs in leaves and most leaves are green (see below).

Plants obtain the carbon dioxide they need from the air around them or, if they are water plants, from air dissolved in water. All land plants and some water plants absorb the water they need through their roots. Some water plants do not need roots to absorb water since they are surrounded by it.

An important by-product of photosynthesis is oxygen. It is important because oxygen is needed by plants and animals for respiration. If there was nothing in the world producing oxygen, life as we know it could not exist. Tropical rain forests release large amounts of oxygen, and this is one of the reasons why it is important to conserve them.

Leaves: the main site of photosynthesis

Photosynthesis can occur in any green part of a plant but most of it occurs in the leaves. Their shape and structure is ideally suited to this function. To maximise the rate of photosynthesis leaves must:

- absorb lots of light – they are usually flat, thin structures and plants have many of them, creating a large surface area for light absorption;
- obtain lots of carbon dioxide – they get this from the air around them through microscopically small holes called stomata (singular: 'stoma') which allow gases to pass into and out of leaves;
- obtain plenty of water – water is absorbed from the soil through the roots. A system of pipe-shaped cells brings water to the leaves. The midrib (see figure 3.2) of a leaf contains some of these tubes and water is distributed around the leaf by the veins which branch off the midrib. Veins also collect the sugar produced by photosynthesis and provide the first link in the transport system which carries sugars and other chemicals to other parts of the plant. Because they are relatively rigid structures, the veins also act as a skeleton which supports the thin leaf blade.

Plant growth

In the early stages of growth all cells are able to divide and all parts of the embryo plant can grow. Later on, growth is restricted to particular areas such as the tips of roots and shoots and special cells in stems and trunks. Plants are only able to grow if they live in places where they can photosynthesise. Their environment must supply them with the raw materials they need for this: water and carbon dioxide, together with enough light energy. They also need a supply of mineral salts for healthy growth.

Plants cannot grow in very cold or very hot conditions. The maximum growth rate occurs in environments like tropical rain forests where there is plenty of water, carbon dioxide and warm temperatures. If conditions are unfavourable, growth may be very slow and sometimes can stop completely. For example, many trees stop growing during the winter when they have shed their leaves. Cacti, which are adapted for life in very hot and dry conditions, have very slow growth rates because of the shortage of water.

REPRODUCTION OF FLOWERING PLANTS

Flowers: organs of sexual reproduction

Flowers contain the sexual reproduction organs of flowering plants. The product of successful sexual reproduction in flowering plants is called an embryo plant. These develop inside structures we call seeds which often develop inside fruits. Making the link between flowers, seeds and fruits is vital when discussing the function of flowers. A good way to do this is to examine the development of fruits on living plants such as the pea. The pea pod, biologically speaking, is the fruit of the pea plant.

Pollination

As discussed on page 4, sexual reproduction requires the coming together of male and female gametes. The male gametes of flowering plants develop inside pollen grains which are formed inside structures called anthers. The female gametes (ovules) are found inside structures called carpels. Before fertilisation can occur the pollen has to be transferred from the anther to a part of the carpel called the stigma: this process is called pollination.

When the word 'flower' is used, most people think of structures with brightly coloured petals and, often, a scent. However, many species of flowering plant, for example all the grasses, have flowers without petals or scent. The structure of a flower depends on the method of pollination which occurs. The bright colours, scent and nectar associated with many flowers attract animals, such as bees and other types of insect, to the flower. On visiting a flower, pollen brushes off the anther on to the body of the animal. When it visits another flower of the same species, some of the pollen may get brushed off on to the stigma of the second flower, thus pollinating it.

Flowers without bright petals or scent are usually pollinated by the wind. Clearly, the wind will blow past a flower regardless of its colour or scent, so wind-pollinated flowers have no need for them. Instead, the anthers and stigmas of wind-pollinated flowers grow in positions that make it more likely that pollen will be blown off or on to them, respectively. Hazel catkins are examples of male flowers that are adapted in this way. Figures 3.3 and 3.4 illustrate the structure of insect- and wind-pollinated flowers.

The reasons for the differences between insect- and wind-pollinated flowers are listed in the box.

Figure 3.3

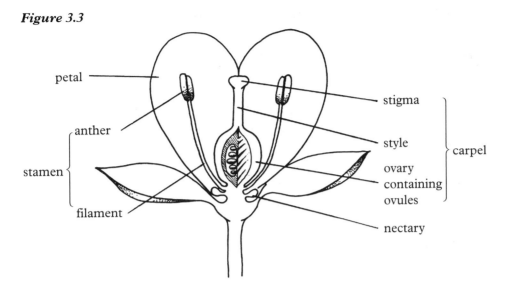

Generalised section through an animal-(e.g. insect-)pollinated flower

Figure 3.4

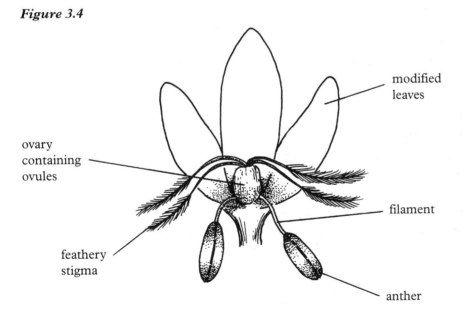

Generalised section through a wind-pollinated grass flower
Note: These flowers are about 3 mm long in common grasses and occur in groups along the ends of the flowering stalks

| Differences between animal- and wind-pollinated plants | |
Animal-pollinated	Wind-pollinated
Brightly coloured petals, scent and nectar to attract animals	No petals, scent or nectar
Anthers and stigmas in positions where animals will brush past them when visiting the flowers	Anthers and stigmas hang outside the flower where they are exposed to the wind
Stigmas produce a liquid to which pollen sticks	Stigmas have a feathery, net-like structure to catch pollen blowing past them
Relatively large, sticky pollen that becomes attached to animals' bodies	Huge numbers of small, light pollen grains which are easily carried away by the wind. This is the type of pollen grain which is reported in the 'pollen count' and is responsible for hay fever

Most species of flowering plant produce flowers which contain both the male and female reproductive organ, but some, such as oak and hazel, have separate male and female flowers on the same plant. In others, such as willow and poplar, male and female flowers are on separate plants.

Fertilisation, seed and fruit formation

When a pollen grain reaches a stigma belonging to a flower of the same species that the pollen came from, a tube grows out of the pollen to the ovule. A male gamete passes down this tube and enters the ovule. Part of the fertilised ovule grows into an embryo plant. Another part develops into a food store. A protective covering grows around these and a seed is formed. In large seeds such as broad beans it is easy to find each of these parts, as illustrated in figure 3.5.

Other parts of the flower then grow into a structure we call a fruit. The word 'fruit' is commonly used to describe things like apples and oranges. The biological use of the term is much wider, including such things as tomatoes, ash 'keys' and sycamore 'helicopters'.

Seed dispersal

Seeds are dispersed away from the parent plant in a variety of ways. As with

Figure 3.5

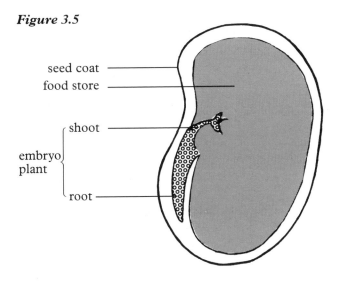

seed coat

food store

shoot

embryo plant

root

Section through a broad bean seed

pollen grains, animals and the wind are the most common means of transport. Apples and tomatoes are examples of fruits which may be eaten by animals. The coat around the seeds prevents them being digested, and intact seeds pass out of the animal in its droppings. Some fruits, for example cleavers, have hook-like structures which attach the fruits to the fur of animals or to clothes. Ash 'keys', sycamore 'helicopters' and dandelion 'parachutes' are all adapted for dispersal by the wind. Dispersal is important because it reduces competition (see page 63) between seedlings and between parent plants and their offspring. As they are spread out they are more likely to start growing in places where the resources they need (water, space and light) are not being used up by other plants.

Seed germination

Three things are essential for germination: water, oxygen and a favourable temperature. Seeds will not germinate at cold temperatures and the germination rate generally increases as the temperature rises, up to a maximum of about 40°C. Above this temperature living processes start being disrupted. Many plants produce seeds in summer and autumn that do not germinate until the following spring. If they did germinate in summer or autumn the young plants would be exposed to the cold winter temperatures and could be killed. Many of these dormant seeds need to be exposed to cold temperatures before they germinate.

THE LIFE-CYCLE OF FLOWERING PLANTS

The life-cycle of a plant comprises the stages that occur as it grows from a seed into a mature plant capable of producing seeds. In flowering plants this always involves pollination, fertilisation, seed production, seed dispersal and germination, as described above.

Annuals

Some species of plant complete their life-cycles in less than one year. These are called annuals; familiar examples are field poppies and sweet peas. Some species, such as groundsel, have such a short life-cycle that they can produce more than one generation in each growing season.

Biennials

Species which require two growing seasons to reach maturity are called biennials. Wallflowers and carrots are examples. In the first season they make food which they store in their root system over the winter. In the spring they use this to grow early in the season. The plant flowers and then dies.

Perennials

Species which can survive for many years are called perennials. All woody plants and some non-woody plants such as daffodils and crocuses are perennials. Daffodils and crocuses survive the winter as underground structures called perennating organs. Daffodils have bulbs, and crocuses produce corms. The woody parts of trees and shrubs survive above ground during winter, but many are deciduous, losing their leaves in autumn and growing new ones in the spring. Evergreen trees and shrubs such as holly keep their leaves during the winter and replace them gradually all through the year.

SUMMARY

- Plants are multi-cellular organisms that can make their own food by photosynthesis. This process involves combining carbon dioxide with water to make a kind of sugar. Oxygen is a by-product of this reaction. Light energy is needed and plants have pigments which absorb light.

Chlorophyll is a green pigment which is essential for photosynthesis, and this is why most plants are mainly green.

- Plants need light, water, air and mineral salts for growth and the maximum rate of growth occurs in warm conditions.
- The plants which are best adapted to life on land are the flowering plants. This group includes trees, shrubs and non-woody plants such as daisies and grasses. All flowering plants have:
  - (a) stems and side-stems (trunks and branches) to support them and transport materials around the plant;
  - (b) roots for anchorage and for absorbing water and mineral salts;
  - (c) leaves for efficient absorption of the light energy needed for photosynthesis;
  - (d) flowers which produce seeds.
- Most flowers are adapted for pollination by either animals or the wind.
- Seeds contain embryo plants and are dispersed away from the parent plants to reduce competition. Animals and the wind are the most common methods of dispersal.
- Seeds need water, oxygen and a favourable temperature to germinate.
- All flowering plants go through a life-cycle which involves pollination, fertilisation, seed production, seed dispersal, germination and growth. Annual plants complete their cycle in less than one year. Biennials take between one and two years. Perennial plants can live for many years.

4

Variation and Classification

ANN GRAHAM AND NIGEL
SKINNER

Introduction   50

Similarities and differences within a
    species   51

Similarities and differences between
    the main groups of animals   51

Similarities and differences between
    the main types of plant groups   55

The naming of living things   56

Identifying living things   57

Summary   58

4
VARIATION AND CLASSIFICATION

ANN GRAHAM
NIGEL SKINNER

INTRODUCTION

Millions of different living things exist. Some are so small that we cannot see them without powerful microscopes; others tower above us. The variations in size, shape, colour and way of life are enormous. The living things that we are most familiar with are animals and plants. Members of the plant kingdom make their own food, usually have green leaves and cannot move from place to place. Members of the animal kingdom feed on plants or on other animals and can move around. These large groups are divided into smaller groups, with similar types being put into the same group. Grouping organisms in this way is called classification.

A group of living things that look very similar to each other and can inter-breed to produce fertile offspring is called a 'species'. There are millions of different species and they are put into larger groupings on the basis of similarities and differences between them. Humans are put into the animal kingdom because we are more similar to other animals than we are to any other type of living thing. We are mammals because, like all other mammals, we have hair on our bodies and give birth to live young which are fed on milk. The mammals we are most similar to are the apes and monkeys. Together with humans these are put into the group called primates.

This chapter discusses the similarities and differences between living things and the ways that they are put into groups. It focuses on:

- similarities and differences within species;
- similarities and differences between the main groups of plants and animals;
- the naming of living things;
- ways of identifying living things.

SIMILARITIES AND DIFFERENCES WITHIN A SPECIES

When we look at people around us it is very obvious that we are all different from one another. There are differences in height, hair colour, shape of nose and so on. Identical twins are more alike than other people but even they have small differences such as different fingerprints. Despite their differences, people are all recognisably human because they share some features in common. Some similarities and differences are listed in the box.

Similarities and differences among humans

Obvious features that humans share with one another	*Some features that vary from person to person*
A head with two eyes, two ears, a nose, a mouth and hair	Colour of hair and eyes
	Language
Two arms with hands and fingers	Shape of ears and nose
Two legs with feet and toes	Height and weight
The ability to walk and run	Size of feet and hands
The ability to communicate using language	Fingerprints
	Speed of running
	Language

Individual members of all other species also vary from one to another. This is not always obvious and it may require careful observations and measurements to find the differences. For example, although all the daisy plants in a lawn may look the same, there will be differences in such things as the length of their flower stalk, the number of leaves, the number of hairs on the leaves, the length of root and so on.

SIMILARITIES AND DIFFERENCES BETWEEN THE MAIN GROUPS OF ANIMALS

Animals are often put into one of two groups, the vertebrates and the invertebrates. Vertebrates all have a vertebral column (sometimes called a backbone) whilst the invertebrates do not. Small invertebrate animals are sometimes called 'minibeasts' but this is not an official classification grouping.

Characteristics of the vertebrates

As well as having a vertebral column, all vertebrates have an internal skeleton made of bone or a tough material called cartilage. They all have two eyes and similarities in their internal structure, e.g. all possess a heart and two kidneys. Despite having these features in common, the vertebrates are a very diverse group that includes animals as different as sharks and elephants. The vertebrate group is divided into five smaller groups called classes. These are the fish, amphibia, reptiles, birds and mammals. The main characteristics of each of these and some examples are listed in the box.

Vertebrate classes		
Name of group (class)	*Main features of the group*	*Familiar examples*
Fish	Scales and fins on the outside of their body. Live in water and lay eggs without shells	Herring, goldfish, trout, sharks, dogfish and skate
Amphibians	A body surface with no scales, sometimes termed 'smooth'. This is misleading because amphibians like toads have a rough surface. They lay eggs without shells in water. Young stages, called tadpoles, live in water and look very different from the adults which can live on land or in water	Frogs, toads and newts
Reptiles	Dry, scaly skin. Lay eggs on land in soft-shelled eggs	Snakes, lizards, alligators, turtles and tortoises
Birds	Body mainly covered with feathers but scales are present on the legs and feet. Beak for feeding. Lay eggs with hard shells on land. Most are able to fly	Robins, ducks, eagles, penguins, flamingos and ostriches
Mammals	Body covered with hair or fur. Give birth to live young which are fed on mother's milk	Elephants, mice, whales, dolphins, kangaroos and humans

Fish, amphibians and reptiles are sometimes called 'cold-blooded' animals whereas birds and mammals are called 'warm-blooded'. These commonly used terms are somewhat misleading. The blood (and body) temperature of 'cold-blooded' animals actually varies in parallel with the temperature of their surroundings. Thus, in cold conditions, the blood and bodies of 'cold-blooded' animals will indeed be 'cold'. However, in warm conditions their blood and bodies become 'warm'.

The blood and body temperature of 'warm-blooded' animals is usually maintained at a relatively constant 'warm' temperature, around 37°C in mammals and 39°C in birds. When mammals hibernate their body temperature falls to a 'cold' 4°C and when they have a fever the temperature may rise slightly. The terms 'cold-blooded' and 'warm-blooded' remain in common usage because their more correct 'scientific' alternatives, 'poikilothermic' and 'homoeothermic' are rather difficult words.

Characteristics of invertebrates

Invertebrate animals do not have a vertebral column or any other bones inside their body. They do, however, possess a skeleton. If they didn't they would have no support for their bodies. There are two main types of invertebrate skeleton. Arthropods, a group which includes insects, spiders, crustacea and myriapods (see below) have an external skeleton. Other invertebrates are sometimes called 'soft-bodied' and their skeleton is a liquid one. This liquid presses against their body walls, thus giving the whole animal shape and rigidity in rather the same way that a balloon is given shape and rigidity when it is filled with air. All invertebrates are 'cold-blooded' or, more correctly, poikilothermic (see above).

There are many invertebrate groups; the main features of the more common groups are described in the box.

Invertebrate classes

Name of group	Main features of the group	Familiar examples
Jellyfish	Tentacles which are used to sting and catch their prey. Body contains much jelly-like material (but they are not fish!). All species are marine	Jellyfish and sea anemones
Segmented worms	Body divided up into ring-shaped sections called segments. Definite 'head' end with mouth. Marine, freshwater and land-living species	Earthworms, leeches and ragworms
Molluscs	Soft bodies which are often protected by a non-living shell. Marine, freshwater and land-living species	Snails, slugs, mussels, limpets and octopuses
Echinoderms ('spiny-skinned' invertebrates)	A hard, spiny body covering and no distinct head. All species are marine	Starfish and sea urchins
Insects	Adults have three pairs of legs and a body divided into three parts: head, thorax and abdomen. The head has eyes and feelers (antennae) and the thorax usually has one or two pairs of wings. Young stages either look similar to the adults and are called nymphs or look very different and are called larvae, caterpillars or grubs. Most species are land-living, some live in freshwater and a few are marine	Beetles, flies, bees, butterflies, fleas, ants and grasshoppers
Arachnids	Divided into two main parts: head and 'body'. Eight legs. Nearly all species are land-living	Spiders, scorpions, mites and ticks
Crustaceans	Body usually covered with hard, chalky plates. Usually five or more pairs of legs for walking or swimming. Most species live in water	Crabs, shrimps, water fleas and woodlice
Myriapods	Have long thin bodies with many legs. Most live in damp places on land	Centipedes and millipedes

SIMILARITIES AND DIFFERENCES AMONG THE MAIN TYPES OF PLANT GROUPS

Plants can be put into one of two groups depending on whether or not they produce seeds.

Plants which produce seeds

Most of the land plants that we are familiar with fall into this group. There are two main groups: flowering plants and conifers.

Flowering plants This group includes organisms as diverse as grasses and trees. All produce flowers which contain their organs of sexual reproduction. The end products of sexual reproduction are seeds which are contained inside fruits. Further details of this group are given in Chapter 3. Most species live on land but a few are adapted to living in water.

Conifers The other familiar seed-bearing plants are the coniferous trees, which do not have flowers but produce their seeds inside cones. All species live on land.

Plants which do not produce seeds

Familiar plants which do not produce seeds fall into three main groups: algae, mosses and ferns.

Algae The algae that we are most familiar with are the seaweeds. These are put into three groups on the basis of their colour: green, red or brown. The red and brown seaweeds do possess the green pigment called chlorophyll which is needed for photosynthesis (see page 40) but other pigments mask its green colour. Most species of algae live in water but a few are adapted to damp conditions on land.

Mosses These are familiar plants in lawns and on trees. They do not grow very tall and can only survive in fairly damp places. They often grow in tufts and this helps them to conserve water. They reproduce by means of spores which develop inside structures called capsules growing up from the plant. Spores are very light, single-celled structures which are dispersed by the wind and can grow into new plants.

Ferns The ferns are better adapted to life on land than mosses are. They can grow much larger than mosses and have stems, roots and leaves (sometimes called fronds) which are similar to those produced by flowering plants. They also produce spores and these can often be seen on the underside of their leaves during the summer and early autumn.

Other 'plants' which produce spores

Fungi Strictly speaking, fungi are not plants because they feed by absorbing nutrients from their surroundings rather than by making their own food by photosynthesis. They are similar to plants since they are unable to move around and, in common with mosses and ferns, produce spores for reproduction. Mushroom spores look like cocoa powder and are produced between the 'gills' underneath their caps.

Lichens These are a very interesting group because they are made up of two completely different kinds of organism. A lichen is an association between a fungus and an alga which benefits both partners.

THE NAMING OF LIVING THINGS

The only groups of living things in which individual members of the group are given individual names are humans, their pets and, occasionally, their domestic animals. Humans can do this because they use language to communicate. It would of course be impossible to give individual names to every individual living thing. Instead, we put all those organisms which look very similar to each other and which can breed with each other to produce fertile offspring into one group that we call a species (see page 50). Biologists give each species a name that is made up of two words derived from the Latin language. The human species is *Homo sapiens*, common daisies are *Bellis perennis* and wrens delight in the name *Troglodytes troglodytes*. By convention the first letter of the first of these names is given a capital letter and both are written in a different style from the text around them, usually in italic script (as above) or by underlining them. This system of naming organisms may seem complicated but it has a number of advantages over the use of local or common names:

● it prevents confusion when the same organism is given a different name in the same country. For example, 'Lords and Ladies', 'Cuckoo Pint' and 'Parson in the Pulpit' are all names used in English for the same species of flowering plant. The Latin name for this species is *Arum maculatum*;

- it enables biologists who do not speak the same language to communicate information about a species, confident that they are both referring to the same type of organism;
- many organisms do not have a common name. For example, what most of us would call a fly could in fact be any one of hundreds of species of organism that comprise the group 'flies';
- sometimes a name in one country is used for a completely different species in another country. For example, a robin in Britain is a completely different species from the North American robin.

IDENTIFYING LIVING THINGS: THE USE OF KEYS

Keys are useful tools for finding out the name of an organism or the group to which it belongs. To use them we need to be able to look at and describe the plant or animal or have a description written down. It is difficult to use a key if you have to depend only on a picture. Keys provide a systematic way of examining a specimen which is more reliable and quicker than flicking through descriptions or photographs in a book. Keys take various forms but the most commonly used are branching (dichotomous) keys. These have mutually exclusive statements arranged in pairs that take the user of the key along different routes, depending on the characteristics of the specimen under observation. The key set out in the box could be used to find out to which class a vertebrate animal belongs.

A key to the five classes of vertebrates

1	Body has scales somewhere on its surface	2
	Body has no scales on it	4
2	Scales cover the majority of the body	3
	Scales only on legs, rest of the body covered in feathers	Birds
3	Has fins	Fish
	Has no fins	Reptiles
4	Has fur or hair on the body surface	Mammals
	Has no fur or hair on the body surface	Amphibia

To explain how this key works, suppose we are trying to find out which classes a cat, a goose, a goldfish, an adder and a frog belong to. It is important to work carefully through the key, considering each pair of statements as you are directed to them.

We start with the first pair of statements and look at all the animals. Only the goose, goldfish and adder are found to have scales somewhere on them; the cat and frog have no scales at all. We go on as directed to the second pair of statements and look only at the goose, goldfish and adder. We find that scales cover the majority of the body surface of the goldfish and adder but are found only on the legs and feet of the goose. The rest of its body is covered with feathers and we can conclude that the goose is a bird while the goldfish and adder are not. We go on to look at the third pair of statements considering only the goldfish and adder. We find that the goldfish has fins and is therefore a fish whilst the adder has no fins and is therefore a reptile.

We have now found out which classes the goose, goldfish and adder are in. Turning our attention back to the cat and the frog, the key directs us from the first pair of statements to the fourth pair. We find that the cat has fur or hair on its body and is therefore a mammal whereas the frog has no fur or hair and is therefore an amphibian.

A good way of learning about how keys work is to construct one for a group of familiar organisms or a group of similar non-living things that differ slightly in shape, colour or size. The key given above is a relatively simple one which does not use complex language. Sometimes keys use descriptive, technical terms which are difficult for non-specialists to understand. Keys used when teaching children need to be chosen carefully to avoid this problem.

SUMMARY

- There are many differences between living things. This is called 'variation'.
- Classification involves putting things into groups on the basis of similarities and differences between them. Those that are most similar are put into the same group.
- The most fundamental of these groups is called a species; it is made up of individuals which share many (but not all) features and can breed with each other to produce fertile offspring.
- Species are given scientific names to avoid the confusion that could occur if only 'common' names were used.
- Keys are tools that are helpful when trying to find out to which group an organism belongs.

5

ANN GRAHAM AND NIGEL SKINNER

Living Things in Their Environment

Introduction	60
The influence of the environment on living things	61
Environmental requirements of living things	63
Plants and animals found in familiar habitats	65
Feeding relationships in ecosystems	69
Micro-organisms	71
Studying plants and animals in their natural environments	74
Sensitive collection of living things	75
Caring for animals in classrooms	75
Studying animals	76
Safety	76
Permission	76
Summary	77

5
LIVING THINGS IN THEIR ENVIRONMENT

ANN GRAHAM
NIGEL SKINNER

INTRODUCTION

This chapter is about the interactions that occur between different types of living thing and between living things and their non-living surroundings. The study of living things in their environment is called ecology. A number of ecological terms are used in this chapter and these are explained below.

The places that organisms live in (their 'homes') are called **habitats**. Habitats can be very different in size, for example both a single oak tree and a lake can be called habitats. All the living things in a habitat make up its **community**. Living things will obviously be affected by the non-living factors around them. These will include things like the temperature and the amount of water, light and space available. A living thing will also be affected by the other living things around it. These could be a source of food or of danger. These living and non-living factors make up the **environment** of a living thing. The term **ecosystem** is used to describe the whole community of living things in a habitat and the way that they interact with their environment. The whole of the Earth together with the living organisms found on it is sometimes thought of as one huge ecosystem called the **biosphere**. The number of a particular type of any living thing in a defined area is called the **population** of that thing. Populations change within ecosystems because of both natural events and human interference. All members of the population need resources such as food, space and water. In any one habitat there are often not enough of such resources to go round. This results in **competition** for them and the 'best' competitors survive at the expense of the 'worst' competitors. **Adaptation** is the term used to describe the ways in which living things are suited to their particular habitats. Those that are well adapted will be better competitors than those which are not. Different adaptations are appropriate in different habitats.

This chapter discusses:

- the ways in which living things are influenced by the environment;
- the things that living things need from their environments;
- the different types of plants and animals likely to be found in places easily available for study and the adaptations these plants and animals show;
- feeding relationships in ecosystems;
- the beneficial and harmful roles that micro-organisms may play in the environment;
- practical points that must be considered when studying plants and animals in their natural habitats.

THE INFLUENCE OF THE ENVIRONMENT ON LIVING THINGS

Among the most obvious factors that affect living things are those associated with the climate. These will include factors such as the temperature, light intensity, amount of rainfall and windspeed.

Temperature

As discussed on page 52 animals are often referred to as either 'cold-blooded' or 'warm-blooded'. Changes in temperature can have a profound effect on cold-blooded animals. Generally, as the temperature drops, these animals move more slowly. In winter, and whenever the temperature is especially low, they hide in cracks in walls or buildings, in holes in the ground, under the bark of a fallen tree or in the mud of a pond. Some may survive the winter as eggs which hatch out in the spring. The temperature underground varies less than that above ground so animals living there may be little affected by seasonal changes. If there is a very hard frost they may be able to move deeper into the soil. In warm weather cold-blooded animals are very active. This is why we see so many flying insects on warm summer days. Many warm-blooded animals are able to survive winter by taking shelter but food is often in short supply so some hibernate and others migrate to warmer places where food is available.

Temperature can affect plants in many different ways. Growth takes place only in the warmer seasons. Many dormant plants such as seeds, bulbs and trees without leaves, need a period of cold weather before they will develop (see page 45). Plants which can flower in the winter, but which are not specially suited to this, may not be able to set seed. Some plants which are described as being 'non-hardy' are killed by frost but most of our common wild plants are hardy. Temperatures, in our climate, are rarely too high for growth to occur, but on very hot days growth may be slowed down because plants are losing too much water and may wilt.

Light intensity

No green plant can grow without light and plants which are short of light tend to grow tall and straggly and have pale green leaves. Some plants, such as those growing in woodland where the trees shed their leaves, overcome the problem of shading by making most of their growth early in the year before the leaves are out on the trees. In many cases, for example bluebells, this is made possible by bulbs or corms which store enough food for this early growth. Some plants can grow well in shade. They are sometimes suited to this by having deep green leaves which trap light very efficiently, for example dog's mercury and ivy.

Rainfall

All animals need water, but since many can move to water if their surroundings dry up, the amount of rain is not very important except in very dry seasons. Then even ponds and streams dry up and when this happens many animals will die.

Rain provides plants with water and this runs into the ground between the soil particles and eventually drains into streams and rivers. Provided there is enough rain, a thin layer of water is held around the soil particles. It is this water that plants can take up through their roots. Soil can become waterlogged if there is too much rain, or if its structure prevents drainage. In this case plant roots may die because they cannot get enough air.

Windspeed

Strong winds occur most often in autumn, winter or early spring when many trees have no leaves. This means that the trees, offering less resistance to the wind, are less likely to be damaged or blown over. Smaller plants can be damaged, but this is less likely because their non-woody stems can bend with the wind.

ENVIRONMENTAL REQUIREMENTS OF LIVING THINGS

To maintain 'life processes' certain things are essential. Living things obviously need to live in places where they can get food, water, air, a space to live and shelter from adverse conditions or danger. Most species of animal and plant produce as many offspring as they can to maximise the chance that some will survive. In natural habitats there is always competition for these sorts of resources.

Feeding in plants

Plants make their own food. To do this they need light, water, carbon dioxide and various other chemicals (see page 40). The competition between plants for light is easy to see. If you look down on most natural habitats that can support life you see very little, if any, bare ground. This is because plants spread out over all surfaces which get light from the sun. Low-growing plants can do this by growing into a rosette or mat shape. At the other extreme are tall trees which, with the help of their woody stems, can stand upright and tower over other plants. Some plants, such as ivy, climb up trees to get to the light and others such as honeysuckle and goosegrass can be seen climbing over hedge plants.

Plants compete for water and mineral nutrients by having root systems that spread through the soil.

Competition for space by plants

One way of competing indirectly for space is to produce a lot of seeds, some of which may land in a suitable place to grow. Some plants grow and spread by underground or overground stems (for example, nettles and creeping buttercup). Some plants need more shelter than others and these will be found growing on the sheltered sides of hedges or walls or under trees. Plants growing in very exposed places such as hillsides often appear to be struggling to survive and may not be able to reproduce there.

Feeding in animals

Animals which feed only on plants are called herbivores. Those that feed only on other animals are called carnivores. Animals which eat other animals are called predators and the animals they feed on are called prey. Some animals are omnivorous and will eat almost anything. Those animals which feed on only one kind of plant or animal are much more at risk from their food supply disappearing. This can be seen with many caterpillars which feed on only one kind of plant and there is often great competition for this food when many eggs are laid together.

Competition for space and shelter in animals

Many animals need shelter from the weather and from predators. We usually think of this in cold, wet or windy weather but many also need to shelter from hot sun and dry conditions in summer. Birds use hedges, trees and outbuildings. Small mammals use holes in the ground or tufts of grass and other plants. Invertebrates can find shelter in compost heaps, in outbuildings, under stones, in pond mud, in pieces of dead wood, underground or around the bases of plants. It may seem surprising to us that these places provide enough shelter, but the weather conditions (for example inside a tuft of grass) may be quite different from the weather we are experiencing higher up. The weather conditions of any tiny area, such as a tuft of grass, are called the microclimate. There is competition among different animals for the most suitable places, and those which do not find shelter are at risk.

A crucial period for finding shelter is the breeding season. Most animals lay eggs or give birth to live young. For many predators, eggs and young animals are particularly good to eat. Some egg-layers, such as ants, wasps, bees and birds, build nests, protect their eggs, and feed and guard their young. However, most invertebrates and larger cold-blooded animals do not guard their eggs or young. Some lay their eggs in as safe a place as they can find. Others lay eggs in very large numbers, so that some will probably survive even if many are eaten. These eggs are usually laid near to a food supply so that when the young hatch they have plenty to eat. For example, cabbage-white butterflies lay their eggs on the backs of cabbage leaves. Frogs lay their eggs in ponds, where the tadpoles will first feed on water weed and later on small animals such as water fleas. Many animals lay their eggs underground to hide them from potential predators and it is common for small mammals to give birth in underground burrows or dens (for example rabbits, badgers and foxes). If young animals hatch or are born in the open, they must be able to run or fly straight away in order to survive.

PLANTS AND ANIMALS FOUND IN FAMILIAR HABITATS

Three habitats likely to be easily available for study are playing fields, gardens and ponds. The main kinds of plant and animal found in these habitats and their adaptations to these places are discussed below.

Playing fields

Most playing fields are originally man-made habitats but, by the time they are ready for use, wild plants and animals will be living there. The way in which the populations of these living things change will depend on how the field is used and looked after. One important point to remember is that many animals can disappear from a habitat by moving away if the conditions are unsuitable. Plants cannot do this and will disappear by dying, or if they are annual plants, by not producing seed.

Plants in playing fields The plants to be found on a playing field will depend on the seed mixture sown, the wear and tear on the field, and on how it is looked after. The most common plants will be grasses and perhaps clovers. The grasses are not usually the ones used on lawns because these are not hard-wearing enough. Instead, rough- and smooth-stalked meadow grass and perennial ryegrass are often found. There will also be some annual grasses such as annual meadow grass which can be found almost everywhere that grass is growing. The clovers are likely to be white clover or the yellow-flowered and more straggly hop trefoil. Once a playing field is in use, bare patches will appear. These will give space for germination and growth to the seeds of other plants which are being blown about by the wind or carried by animals. Very many different kinds of plants can colonise these patches. The most common are daisy, cat's ear, hawkbit, creeping buttercup, germander speedwell, ribwort, plantain and various mosses. Many of the plants will not flower because of the frequent mowing and wear from being trodden on. This can make identification difficult but it is possible to identify some kinds from the shape of their leaves. If weedkillers are used there may be only very few plants with broad leaves.

Animals in playing fields There are often few animals to be seen on the surface of a playing field but there will probably be signs of animals such as worm casts, rabbit droppings, mole hills, birds' feathers and, in some weather conditions, footprints and tracks. Many of these are signs of visitors rather than animals which live in the field. Most resident animals live below ground. Examples include many invertebrates such as earthworms, ants, beetles, slugs, woodlice, snails, millipedes, centipedes and insect larvae such as leatherjackets and wireworms. It is possible to remove and then replace turf in order to look for these animals without damage to the field. As with broad-leaved plants, differences will be found in the numbers of animals in different parts of the field due to trampling.

Adaptations to living in playing fields Plants growing on a playing field must be able to survive frequent mowing and being trampled on. Grasses are particularly well adapted because their growing points are at the bottom of the leaves instead of at the tip of the shoots so plants can continue to grow when their tips are cut or broken off. Grasses also produce a number of new shoots at ground level without growing taller. This means that individual grass plants can spread quickly over the ground. Most other plants found on playing fields are low growing so they are not cut off by the mower. Trampling harms plant shoots and compresses the soil, which means that water tends to stay on the surface in puddles. Plants which survive in such places usually have rosette forms of growth, for example daisy, cat's ear and ribwort plantain. Alternatively they spread over the surface producing a mat, like creeping buttercup and some creeping grasses.

Most of the animals living on or under a playing field or visiting it are likely to be finding their food there. Some will be feeding on plants, for example rabbits and aphids on the leaves and leatherjackets on the roots. Some will be eating other animals, for example blackbirds eating worms and spiders eating flies, while others such as woodlice will be feeding on dead plants. Any which live on the surface of the ground need protection against being eaten. Some are camouflaged (for example grasshoppers and aphids). Others may taste unpleasant and advertise this by being brightly coloured, for example lady-birds. Some mimic an animal which is dangerous, for example hover flies (which are harmless) have orange and black markings and look very much like wasps. Surface-living animals also need protection against drying up and this often consists of a waterproof covering which can be easily seen on many insects (for example beetles). Animals like earthworms which do not have a waterproof covering can only live in damp conditions. If the surface layers of the soil dry out they move down into deeper layers. The body shape of animals that live in the soil is often well suited to moving through the soil because it is long, thin and pointed: worm-shaped in fact!

Alternative habitats If a playing field is not available, suitable alternatives are a farmer's grazed field or an area of common land, both of which are likely to contain many more kinds of plants and animals than a playing field. Many fields are surrounded by hedges or stone walls and these are very interesting habitats to study.

Gardens

Gardens can be very varied habitats depending on how they are looked after, which plants are grown and to what extent poisonous chemicals are used.

Cultivated gardens A vegetable, fruit or flower garden which is regularly weeded and in which pesticides are used will only contain the plants which have been deliberately sown or planted and few resident animals except those below ground. These will be the same kinds as those listed for the playing field, except that there will be larger numbers because the soil will contain more plant and animal waste (organic matter) and is likely to be better drained. There will be visiting animals including bees, wasps, flies, butterflies, moths, birds and perhaps mice, hedgehogs and toads.

Wild gardens A wild garden or corner of a garden with perhaps a compost heap and some pieces of rotting wood is a habitat with more favourable conditions for a wider variety of plants and animals. Many of the plants will have spread from neighbouring areas by seeds or underground and overground stems. Plants such as bindweed, nettles, dead-nettles, ground elder, couch grass, creeping thistle and creeping buttercup can spread in this way. Plants which spread readily from seed include trees such as sycamore and ash, dandelions, groundsel, thistles and docks. Seeds can remain dormant in the soil for many years and may germinate when the soil is turned over and they are brought near the surface.

Wild gardens can provide habitats for many more species of animal than well-tended gardens. Insects such as aphids, ladybirds, butterflies, moths and beetles together with other invertebrates like spiders, woodlice and centipedes will find suitable places to live. There will also be more species of bird, and other vertebrates may include hedgehogs, mice, voles, grey squirrels, toads and grass snakes.

Adaptations to living in gardens Gardens are usually very pleasant habitats with good supplies of a variety of foods. In a cultivated garden a plant will be more welcome if it looks nice, smells nice or is known to be good to eat, because then the gardener is less likely to pull it out! In a wild garden the successful plants will be those which are the best competitors.

The numbers and types of animals will depend on the food available, and on the gardener. He or she may try to kill animals which are feeding on and harming the attractive and useful plants. In so doing, other harmless or beneficial animals may also be killed. The overall effect may be to take away the food supply of many animals, so greatly reducing the variety found. If, for example, all the aphids are killed there will be no food for the ladybirds and a whole food chain will be disrupted (see page 70).

Alternative habitats Habitats which can be used as alternatives to gardens are patches of waste ground, rubbish dumps, roadsides and disused railway lines. These need to be looked at carefully before taking children to them as they can be dangerous places. Parks may have areas similar to playing fields and suitable for study but their gardens are usually too well tended to provide much of interest.

Ponds

A pond is a much more specialised habitat than those so far described.

Plants in and around ponds Plants such as reeds, rushes, sedges and irises may be found growing round the edges; others such as duckweed will be floating on the surface of the water. Some plants, such as water lilies and many pondweeds, will be rooted at the bottom, and a few such as Canadian pondweed may be floating free. Other plants often found near natural ponds are marsh marigolds, brooklime, water crowfoot, hogweed, water parsnip and water dropwort.

Animals in and around ponds There are several different animal habitats in and around a pond. Frogs may be living in damp areas round the edges. Pondskaters, gnats, mosquito larvae and water boatmen, among others, will be found on or just below the surface of the water. Entirely in the water there may be small fish, tadpoles in early spring, water fleas, flatworms, leeches, pond snails, water beetles and fresh-water shrimps. Living on the bottom you may find dragonfly nymphs and caddis fly larvae.

Adaptations to pond life Plants which live in water do not need strong stems because the water supports them. Some have stems containing large air spaces, which both help the plants to float and also supply air for respiration. Many water plants have very poor roots or no roots at all. Nutrients are absorbed through underwater leaves which are usually feathery and can look very different from the large surface leaves. Most water plants do not depend on setting seed in order to reproduce. Instead, they spread by long underground or overground stems or other normal plant parts which break off and grow into new plants. This is a form of asexual reproduction called vegetative reproduction and it allows plants (such as duckweed) to spread quickly. The process can be watched in the classroom if a few duckweed plants are floated on the surface of some pond water. Each plant will be seen to produce a new plantlet, consisting of a leaf and tiny root, which separates from the parent. Many of the plants which live at the edges of ponds (such as reeds) have long creeping underground stems which push through the mud and hold the plants upright. Others cope with the wet conditions by growing in thick clumps which prevent the shoots from sinking into the mud, for example rushes and some sedges.

For animals, the greatest problem of living in water is getting enough oxygen. Many use the oxygen from the air which is dissolved in the water and this is why running water (which contains more dissolved air) is a better habitat for many animals than a still pond. Many water animals (such as flatworms, water fleas and midge larvae) have very thin skins through which the oxygen can pass. Fish, tadpoles, dragonfly nymphs and caddis fly larvae have special structures called gills which have a large surface area for absorbing oxygen. Others, like mosquito and gnat larvae, water boatmen and beetles, have special breathing tubes which they use to collect air from just above the pond surface. Many animals have more than one method of getting air, for example snails usually collect air from the surface but can get it through their skin if the pond is frozen over.

Some animals have special methods of feeding which make them suitable for living in water, for example water fleas are filter feeders and strain small particles of food out of the water.

Alternative habitats Alternative habitats to a pond are a stream or lake; they are likely to have a greater variety of animals and plants than the pond.

FEEDING RELATIONSHIPS IN ECOSYSTEMS

Almost all of the animals and plants on the Earth depend on the sun for their food. This is because sunlight energy is essential for the process of photosynthesis, as described on page 40. The organic matter made by plants is food for animals, which in turn may be food for other animals. Because plants make their food they are all termed 'producers'. All animals are called 'consumers' because they consume plants or other animals. There is a flow of food (and therefore energy) from producers to consumers.

Food chains

The feeding relationships in an ecosystem can be shown diagrammatically as a food chain. Plants are first in the chain, then animals which feed on plants, then animals which feed on other animals, and so on. The final animal in the chain is known as a top predator. In the previous section, three ecosystems were taken as examples suitable for study. In each of these several different food chains will occur. A feature of food chains is that there are very many different plants which can start a chain, many herbivores which eat plants, fewer carnivores which eat the herbivores and only very few top predators. Humans, who eat meat, are top predators along with birds of prey, foxes and badgers. However, humans rarely eat carnivores (except for some fish and free-range poultry which feed on worms and insects as well as grain) and therefore food chains involving them are often shorter than those involving other animals.

Examples of food chains from a number of different ecosystems are shown below.

Playing field:
GRASS → APHID → BEETLE → SPARROW → OWL

Garden:
LETTUCE → SNAIL → THRUSH → BUZZARD

Pond:
PONDWEED → MIDGE LARVA → GOLDFISH → HERON

Wood:
OAK TREE → CATERPILLAR → BLUE TIT → SPARROWHAWK

Farm:
GRASS → SHEEP → HUMAN

MICRO-ORGANISMS

Micro-organisms (also called microbes) are found almost everywhere on Earth. Most are too small to be seen even with a magnifying glass. We can tell that they are around us because we can see (and sometimes feel or smell) the results of their activities. They have the same basic needs as other living things but there are many different kinds which can be recognised in different ways. Some are minute animals or plants but many do not fit into either of these groups. These are the bacteria, the microscopic fungi (moulds and yeasts) and the viruses. The last group do not even consist of a cell and have to enter the cell of another organism to reproduce.

Harmful microbes

Some microbes make us or animals ill, others harm our plants and others spoil our food, rot the wood in our buildings or discolour paintwork.

Most of those which make us or our animals ill are bacteria or viruses. They get inside our bodies and do damage which makes us have a fever, a rash, an upset tummy or perhaps a runny nose or cough. Examples of illnesses caused by viruses are influenza, the common cold, measles and chicken pox. Most viruses can infect only one kind of animal so the virus diseases which animals can get are caused by different viruses although the symptoms of the diseases they cause may be similar. Examples are distemper in dogs, cat influenza and foot-and-mouth disease in cattle. There are very few drugs which can kill viruses and if recovery from a viral disease occurs it is usually without any medical treatment. For many of the common microbial diseases there are vaccines available which can give immunity to the disease. No vaccine is available for some viral diseases (e.g. the common cold) because the viruses which cause the diseases keep changing slightly. All that can be done is to treat the symptoms by, for example, taking pain-killing drugs such as aspirin or paracetamol. Bacterial diseases of humans and animals include some kinds of food poisoning, tuberculosis, tetanus and some kinds of pneumonia. Many bacterial infections can be cured by antibiotics.

Some of the hardest diseases to prevent or cure are those caused by minute single-celled organisms called protozoans. These diseases are most common in hot countries and include malaria, sleeping sickness and some types of dysentery.

A few types of moulds and yeasts can cause diseases such as athlete's foot, thrush and ringworm (which is *not* caused by a worm). These infections are not usually serious but can be difficult to cure.

Diseases of plants are most often caused by moulds or viruses. Common mould diseases are mildews, wilts and rusts which, even if they do not kill the plants, may make them so weak that they do not produce food for us. Virus diseases often turn the leaves yellow or mottled and reduce the rate at which the plant can photosynthesise. All our food, unless it has been heated strongly in a closed container, will contain bacteria, yeasts and moulds. If warmth and moisture is available (together with air for moulds) they will multiply, causing the food to look and taste unpleasant. Such food may also be dangerous to eat because some of the microbes can cause food poisoning.

Beneficial microbes

Most types of microbe are harmless and many of them are very beneficial. We make use of them to preserve some foods (e.g. in cheese and yoghurt making), to make some drinks (e.g. beer and cider), to make chemicals and to get rid of waste.

When a living thing dies its body contains many nutrients. If these remained inside it, the Earth would rapidly become short of nutrients and there would be an ever-increasing number of dead bodies of plants and animals. This does not happen because there is a cycling of matter in which the dead bodies rot and their nutrients are made available for reuse by other living things. Live animals all produce wastes consisting of undigested food (faeces) and substances which are the waste products of the activities of their bodies. These are also broken down and recycled, together with other things which have been alive (e.g. a cabbage leaf) or have been made from materials which were once alive (e.g. paper) that we throw away. This breaking down is called rotting, and things which rot cause no harm to the environment provided there are not too many of them.

Cycling in communities

In a wood the producers (trees and other plants, see page 70) take in carbon dioxide from the air and water and dissolved mineral nutrients such as nitrates from the soil. These substances are built into the bodies of the plants as carbon compounds and proteins. Some of the plant material will be eaten by animals (the consumers) and some of these animals will be eaten by other animals. In the autumn, when many trees lose their leaves and the annual plants die, this dead organic matter will begin to rot due to the action of organisms collectively called decomposers. Animal wastes and any dead animals also rot. When this happens, the carbon from the carbon compounds becomes carbon in carbon dioxide and enters the air again and the proteins are broken down to form nitrates in the soil.

The carbon cycle

Carbon is taken from the air as carbon dioxide and used by green plants in photosynthesis to make organic matter, which becomes part of the bodies of plants or animals. Some of this is broken down by respiration processes (see page 6) in plants and animals. This process releases carbon dioxide back to the air. Other carbon compounds stay inside the plant and animal bodies until they die and rot when they too are changed into carbon dioxide. Another important source of carbon dioxide in the air comes from the burning of fossil fuels. These are coal, oil and natural gas that were formed from plants millions of years ago. The carbon cycle is shown diagrammatically in Figure 5.1.

Figure 5.1

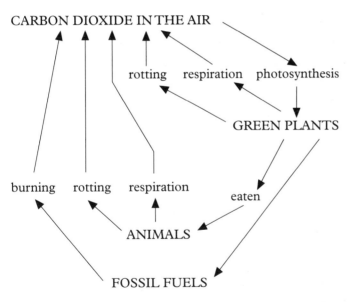

The carbon cycle

The nitrogen cycle

The nitrogen cycle is more complicated than the carbon cycle because nitrogen is found in so many different compounds. There is a lot of nitrogen in the air but only a little of it enters the nitrogen cycle because plants cannot take in gaseous nitrogen. Only a few specialised microbes can do this. Some of these live in the soil and others live in lumps called nodules which they cause on the roots of some plants. The main plants which can have these nodules are peas, beans, lupins, clovers and other legumes. Other types of soil-living microbe can return nitrogen to the air. Most plants take up their nitrogen as nitrates from the soil. When the plants and animals die and rot, the nitrogen is returned to the soil where still other microbes turn it back into nitrates which the plants can use. This cycle is illustrated in Figure 5.2.

Figure 5.2

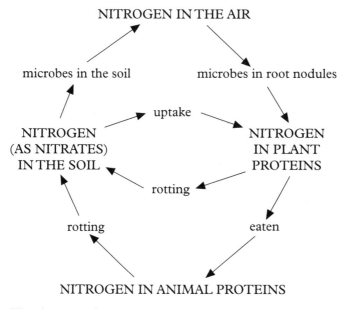

The nitrogen cycle

STUDYING PLANTS AND ANIMALS IN THEIR NATURAL ENVIRONMENTS

The presence of a human in or near a habitat is bound to affect the ecosystem. Care has to be taken when studying a habitat to disturb the animals and plants as little as possible. The 1981 Wildlife and Countryside Act lists those animals and plants which are protected and must not be collected or picked. Apart from ponds, the habitats suggested for study in this chapter are those in which humans are often interfering, so visits by children will have little extra effect. However, children need to be taught to respect all living things and encouraged not to make value judgements about them. Many children will have seen people pulling up 'weeds' and killing 'pests', but in biological terms these are just plants and animals in the wrong place for human convenience. They are living where they are because the environment suits them.

SENSITIVE COLLECTION OF LIVING THINGS

Animals which are protected by law must never be collected. However, many invertebrates such as woodlice, snails, slugs, earthworms and many insects are plentiful in a range of habitats, and little harm can come from taking them into the classroom for a time. Such animals may be collected by gentle sieving of soil, by using pooters (devices which suck in small animals) or by using nets. Care must be taken not to damage the animals, particularly when emptying pooters and nets. Gentle tapping is the best way of persuading animals to move from one container to another. When pond dipping, the contents of the nets should be immediately transferred to a bucket of pond water before perhaps putting the animals into dishes of water for closer study.

Plants which are not protected by law can be collected but it is advisable to pick only ones which are both common and plentiful. Even then it should rarely be necessary to pick more than one of any species. The roots of wild plants should never be dug up.

CARING FOR ANIMALS IN CLASSROOMS

Land animals

Earthworms, woodlice, snails and slugs all feed on living or dead plant material. They can be kept in an aquarium tank with a little soil and plenty of dead and living leaves, provided a little water is sprayed into the tank from time to time. Carnivores should be kept separate from other animals which they may eat and it is better not to keep them overnight because of the difficulty of feeding them. The carnivores most likely to be collected are various beetles, centipedes, some kinds of ants and spiders.

Pond animals

Pond animals, particularly pond snails, can be kept in an aquarium with pondweed. It is best to fill the aquarium with pond water rather than tap water. If this is not available, rainwater is suitable. The water should be changed frequently and it may be necessary to use an aquarium pump to aerate the water.

STUDYING ANIMALS

Children should be discouraged from handling any animals too much and instead be encouraged to think about their well-being. Animal behaviour should be watched under conditions which are as natural as possible. It is acceptable to mark snail shells with a dab of paint in order to try to track their movements (in, for example, a garden) but most other animals are best left as little disturbed as possible. Very active animals can be slowed down a little by placing them in a refrigerator (*not a freezer*) for a few minutes. This will do them no harm and may allow them to be examined closely without killing them.

SAFETY

When taking children outside to work it is important to consider the safety aspects. Some plants and animals are poisonous to the touch and can cause painful skin rashes, stings or bites. The most obvious ones to look out for are nettles, ants, bees, wasps and, when at a pond, hogweed, water dropwort and water boatmen. It is best to discourage children from handling animals, and to provide them with disposable gloves for handling plants, particularly in areas likely to have been fouled by dogs or cats. Thorough hand-washing is essential after such work.

PERMISSION

If the school grounds cannot provide the habitats for study, it is necessary to get written permission from landowners or local authorities to use private or public sites.

SUMMARY

- Habitats are places where animals and plants live and therefore they must supply all the needs of living things. Most importantly these are food, shelter and a place to reproduce.
- Each habitat differs in the way in which it supplies these necessities and therefore animals and plants will be particularly suited to the habitat in which they live.
- Some habitats are more suitable than others for a wider range of plants and animals, and in these there will probably be greater competition between different kinds.
- In every habitat there will be predators and prey, and the population of a predator will be related to the population of its prey.
- All habitats will be affected by factors such as their geographical position, weather conditions, the time of day and the season of the year.
- The interactions between these factors and the living things and between the living things themselves make up an ecosystem.
- Green plants are the only producers of their own food on Earth, and all animals either eat plants or other animals or both. This can be shown in diagrammatic form as a food chain.
- All organic waste material from living things and dead bodies of plants and animals rot due to the action of micro-organisms provided there is air, moisture and a suitable temperature. This rotting prevents the build-up of dead bodies and wastes.
- Some micro-organisms are also responsible for a variety of diseases in plants and animals.

GEOFFREY WICKHAM

Introduction   80

Solid objects   80

Magnetic behaviour   82

Electrical conductivity   82

Natural or synthetic?   83

Solids, liquids and gases   84

Heating substances   87

Burning   88

The water cycle   89

Dissolving   89

Separating mixtures   91

Summary   92

6

Materials and Their Properties

6
MATERIALS AND THEIR PROPERTIES

GEOFFREY WICKHAM

INTRODUCTION

This branch of the syllabus deals with the exploration of the material world: the world of solids, liquids and gases. To the scientist, copper and talcum powder, lemonade and shampoo, air and natural gas are all materials. (There might be confusion here where pupils have heard the word 'materials' applied only to cloth and fabrics.) Pupils' investigation of these will later lead to the idea of matter being made of small particles: atoms and molecules. The ideas of physical and chemical changes are explored, and the possibility of creating new materials from naturally occurring ones.

While the stress is on pupils' investigations, for reasons of safety these must be selected, guided and closely supervised. For example, an instruction to investigate common liquids found in the home could safely include non-alcoholic drinks (if not hot), washing-up liquid, toiletries and soups. However, left to their own devices, pupils might find strong acids (battery acid), strong alkalis (oven cleaner), bleaches, solvents and inflammable liquids (petrol and paraffin). Some of these could cause blindness if splashed in the eyes, or burn skin, or give off harmful vapours. None of the above hazardous substances is suitable for primary school children to handle.

SOLID OBJECTS

Children need to be able to sort objects into different categories. This is like the children's game in which you have to identify objects by touch alone. The objects are placed in a bag so that you cannot see them: you can only put your hand in the bag and feel them.

When you first touch an object there are two immediate sensations. Children may say that some objects in the bag feel colder than others, and this might need some explanation. All the objects in the bag are, in fact, at the same temperature, but some materials carry heat away better than others. These will carry heat from your hand more quickly than other materials and so feel colder. Metals carry heat more quickly than wood, so metals feel colder than wood, even though the metal and the wood are at the same temperature. We say that materials which carry heat quickly are **heat conductors** (or **thermal conductors**) while those which do not are **thermal insulators**.

The other touch sensation is texture. We can categorise objects broadly as smooth, rough, hairy, furry and so on. In fact, our ability to distinguish objects by their texture exceeds our ability to describe the sensation. So, by touch, it is not difficult to distinguish between blotting paper, newspaper, brown wrapping paper and the glossy paper used for colour supplements.

Touching an object gives you some information about it, but you can get even more by holding it. This will give an indication of its weight. You will also be able to tell something about its hardness (or 'scratchability') and elasticity (or springiness). Many objects will be completely hard, as far as your hands can tell, but not all of these will have the same elasticity. A steel ball-bearing, dropped on a tiled floor, will bounce. That is, it will deform and then spring back rapidly to its former shape. It is springy. A china cup will not bounce: it will just shatter. It too is hard, but whereas metals are springy some hard substances like china are brittle. Some soft objects like tennis balls also bounce by being distorted and then rapidly returning to their former shapes. Objects that are even softer, like tomatoes, might regain their shape too slowly to bounce, or like lumps of putty or plasticine they may keep the shape into which they have been pressed. They have no springiness: that is, no elasticity.

Children sometimes confuse 'hardness' and 'weight', possibly thinking of the effect, for example, of dropping a lump of metal on a toe. The two are quite different. For example, lead is a heavier metal than iron (in other words, a given volume of lead weighs more than the same volume of iron), but lead is much softer than iron. It is much easier to scratch the surface of lead with a penknife than to scratch iron.

Looking at something gives you more information about the object, the most obvious being colour. In addition there are the various ways in which materials reflect or transmit light. An eggshell reflects a lot of the light that falls on it, but, because its surface is so rough, it looks matt or dull. As a surface becomes more polished it reflects light in a more regular way so that, like glass or polished metals, it becomes mirror-like. All metals, when polished, have a distinctive shiny appearance, although many, like lead, tarnish very quickly.

Some substances let light pass through them. Glass and diamond are transparent, but other materials like frosted glass and thin bone china are translucent: you cannot see through them but they do let light through. Two other properties of materials can only be investigated by simple experiments: they are magnetic behaviour and electrical conductivity.

MAGNETIC BEHAVIOUR

If you touch some materials with a magnet there is an obvious attraction. Some small objects, like pins, can be lifted up with a magnet. All such objects will be metals, but not all metals will be attracted. The only metals which are attracted by magnets are iron and steel (which is mainly iron), nickel and cobalt. The last two are unlikely to be met very often, so it is a fairly safe bet to say that if a magnet attracts a metal, that metal is iron or steel.

ELECTRICAL CONDUCTIVITY

This can be investigated with fairly simple apparatus: a torch battery, a torch bulb, and a few pieces of plastic-covered wire. Connect it up as shown in Figure 6.1. (The bulb is easiest to connect when screwed into a holder with

Figure 6.1

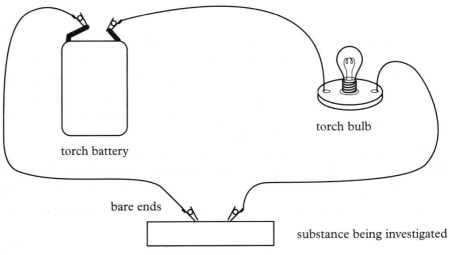

Investigating electrical conductivity

terminals, obtainable from suppliers of school laboratory equipment, and the wires are easier to connect if small crocodile clips are attached.)

Check that the bulb lights when the two bare ends of wire are touched together. Then with the two bare ends touch the material you are investigating. If the bulb lights, the material has carried (conducted) electricity from one bare end to the other. The material is a conductor of electricity. All metals are electrical conductors. The only solid non-metal that conducts electricity to any great extent is graphite, a material used in pencil lead.

NATURAL OR SYNTHETIC?

In our daily lives we are surrounded by, and use, a vast number of different materials, many of which occur naturally, like stone, wood and wool. However, a large number of the materials we use, like plastics and synthetic fibres, reflect the ingenuity of the human race down the centuries.

The first humans used the materials they could find to build shelters, and in this respect resembled the animal kingdom, nest-building being a common animal activity.

The great step forward, where the human differs from other animals, is in deliberately creating new materials. So, where stones were unavailable, bricks were made by shaping mud into blocks and letting them dry in the sun. These bricks had the advantage over stones of being easy to stack in neat rows, but while in a new shape they were still recognisably dried mud. The process was improved by baking the blocks in an oven, causing chemical changes, so that the bricks were no longer a natural product.

In the same way, glass is not a substance that is found in nature, but is a synthetic material. One story credits the ancient Phoenicians with having invented glass by a happy accident when they landed on a sandy shore and could find no stones to support their cooking pots over a fire. They were carrying a cargo of blocks of washing soda, so used these to support the pots. After the fire had died down they found lumps of a transparent glassy material where the soda had been in contact with the sand. What they had produced was a synthetic material: one which does not occur naturally. Glass is still made by the same basic process: strongly heating in a furnace a mixture of soda, sand and limestone.

The search for an artificial stone led the Romans to invent a material which could be used to bind stones together: cement. Some of their cement can still be seen in the Roman lighthouse at Dover, and in parts of the London Wall in the grounds of the Tower of London. In its modern form, cement is made by strongly heating chalk and clay together. When this cement is mixed with stone and sand it produces a very strong substance called concrete which hardens with age.

Materials like glass and concrete, and alloys (mixtures of metals) such as brass and bronze, have been known for so long that we tend to forget that they are 'synthetic' as opposed to natural products. The word 'synthetic' usually conjures up materials produced by the chemical industry.

The birth of the oil industry made available a whole range of new chemicals which could be converted into plastics. So wide is the range that plastics can be designed to give any properties that are needed. Look round the average classroom and you will see a large number of different plastics, all with properties that suit their uses. Some are very hard and strong, like light-switch covers and plastic furniture; others are light and flexible, like disposable plastic beakers and most packaging materials. Their water-resisting properties have made them useful for water pipes, sinks and washing-up bowls. When made in the form of a solid foam (such as expanded polystyrene) they have heat-insulating properties. The thick, soft-feeling plastic beakers are an example of this, and they are also used for house insulation and for packaging.

The use of so many plastic materials has meant that, while using up precious reserves of oil, some of the world's other rare resources can be saved, since plastics are now used where metals and wood once were the only materials available. Car bumpers, for example, are nearly all plastic now, whereas they always used to be chromium-plated steel. All of the early television sets had wooden cases: nearly all are now plastic.

One of the main disadvantages of plastics has been the difficulty of recycling them, because they do not naturally decompose easily, and burning them produces all sorts of harmful and poisonous gases. As a result great efforts have been made to develop plastics which will slowly rot away when no longer needed: these are called biodegradable plastics.

SOLIDS, LIQUIDS AND GASES

A block of wood is solid, and water is liquid: we can see and feel them, and it is not difficult to put the differences between them into words. Solids have a definite volume and a definite shape, even soft solids like modelling clay and jelly, although their shapes can easily be altered by shaping or squeezing. Liquids have a definite volume but no definite shape. They take up the shape of the container they are in. Liquids are obviously 'runny', that is, they can be poured. How do you then answer the question: 'Salt can be poured from a salt cellar, so is it a liquid?'

Grains of salt can be felt to be solid, but can slide over each other. Similarly tennis balls are obviously solid but could be poured out of a bucket. At the other extreme, grains of talcum powder are almost too small to be seen without a magnifying glass but are also solid. The smaller the particles, the more like a liquid the substance becomes. Scientists believe that all materials (solid, liquid or gas) are made of particles we call atoms. What does this suggest about the size of the atoms in a liquid?

The idea of air as a gas is more difficult: it cannot be seen or touched, although on a windy day it can be felt. Children can also be confused because the word 'gas' is often used to refer to the one particular gas supplied by the gas company for cooking and heating.

The real nature of air as a gas can be felt by putting a finger over the end of a bicycle pump full of air and pressing the handle. You will be able to press it so far and no further. Air does not have a fixed volume, like solids and liquids. It can be compressed, which is why it is used in car and bicycle tyres, making them bouncy. If it is not enclosed any gas will spread and fill up all the available space.

Gases do have weight, but are much lighter than the same volume of liquid or solid. An 'empty' milk bottle contains about half a gramme of air, and the air in the average living room of a house weighs about as much as a person. (In reply to a child's inevitable question of how big a room, how heavy a person, the air in a room 4 m × 4 m × 3 m weighs about 57 kg, or 9 stone.)

The particles in solids, liquids and gases

We have just compared the differences between solids, liquids and gases, called the three 'states' of materials. The three states contain exactly the same particles, but arranged in different ways. Water, for example, can exist as ice, water and steam, totally different in appearance, but each containing the same particles. In the same way, most materials can exist in the form of solid, liquid and gas (see Figure 6.2).

The particles in ice are packed tightly together and held by strong forces. As a result they cannot leave their positions, but only vibrate to and fro (Figure 6.2(a)). Any solid in which these particles are in a regular fixed

Figure 6.2

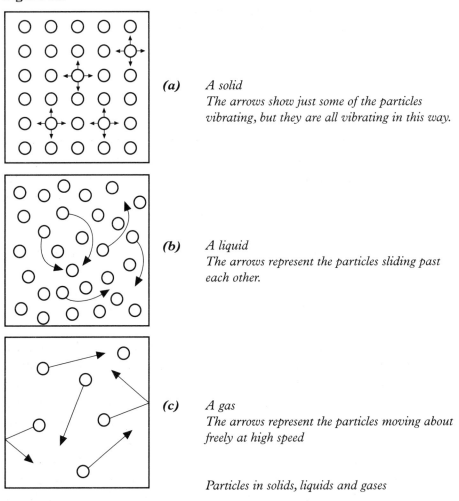

(a)   *A solid*
*The arrows show just some of the particles
vibrating, but they are all vibrating in this way.*

(b)   *A liquid*
*The arrows represent the particles sliding past
each other.*

(c)   *A gas*
*The arrows represent the particles moving about
freely at high speed*

Particles in solids, liquids and gases

pattern will be crystalline (like frost crystals). If the solid is not crystalline the particles will be in a random arrangement.

When ice is heated, the strong forces between the particles become weaker, and the particles become free to move and slide past each other, even though they are still close together (Figure 6.2(b)). So the ice melts and becomes a liquid. There are still forces holding the particles together, but they are weaker than in a solid.

More heat will warm the water up until it boils, when the liquid becomes a gas: steam. The particles in steam are far apart and moving at high speed (Figure 6.2 (c)). They might collide with each other, but there are almost no forces holding them together.

The 'particles' referred to in the case of water are water 'molecules'. A molecule is a group of atoms bound together, but there is no need to distinguish between atoms and molecules at this stage.

HEATING SUBSTANCES

An ice cube placed on a hotplate will melt into water and then boil away as steam. This is called a physical change because ice, water and steam are basically the same substance but in different physical states: solid, liquid and gas. Also these changes can be reversed, because when the steam meets a cold window pane it condenses back to water which, placed in a freezer, will turn back to ice.

Many substances follow this pattern, although the temperatures are often outside our everyday experience. Iron, for example, melts to become liquid, or molten iron, at 1 536°C and boils to become gaseous iron at 2 750°C. Oxygen gas turns to liquid oxygen if cooled to –183°C and becomes solid oxygen at –214°C.

For every pure substance like water, iron or oxygen there is a definite temperature at which these changes take place. For many others the changes are more gradual: substances like glass, chocolate, wax and jelly soften as they are heated so that between solid and liquid comes what could either be regarded as a very soft solid or a very thick (viscous) liquid. In all the above cases a physical change has happened. The material has changed from one state to another: from solid to liquid, and from liquid to gas. However, the substance is still the same chemical so no chemical change has taken place. Molten glass is chemically the same substance as solid glass. All these changes can be reversed by cooling them down.

A sugar cube placed on a hotplate will first melt. At this stage it could still be cooled back to solid sugar. With further heating the syrupy liquid will turn brown and smell of caramel, and will then give off steam and leave a black solid mass. What started as one pure substance has now broken down to become at least two different substances: carbon and water. The sugar has decomposed and cannot easily be converted back to the original substance: this has been a chemical change in which the sugar has broken down mainly to carbon (the black solid mass) and water (in the form of steam). Sugar is one chemical substance, and carbon and water are two totally different chemicals; so a chemical change has happened to get from one substance to the others. This change is called a chemical reaction.

Wood and bread are other materials based mainly on carbon and water which break down to black masses, charcoal and burnt toast respectively.

Pure substances which can be broken down to give other substances are called **compounds**. Sugar is a compound, and so is water. Water cannot be broken down by heating, but more complicated methods will break it down into two gases, oxygen and hydrogen. These two gases can react together explosively to produce water.

There are substances which cannot be broken down by heat or any chemical process into any simpler chemical. These substances are called **elements**. Carbon, oxygen, hydrogen and iron are examples of elements.

Many common processes involving heat are chemical reactions. Baking a cake is one example, even though it involves a mixture of many complex ingredients, like butter and flour, rather than just pure compounds. The finished product is no longer recognisable as a mixture of flour, butter and so on, and there is no way in which the process can be reversed to give the separate ingredients again. In a similar way the baking of clay to make pottery is a chemical process.

Any process which cannot be easily reversed is likely to be a chemical process. Yoghurt cannot be converted back into milk, nor bread into dough: yoghurt-making and the baking of bread are chemical processes.

To summarise: changes in which the substance is essentially the same substance after the change, but in a different state, are called **physical changes**. Physical changes can be reversed: water can be turned to ice, and ice to water.

Changes in which new substances are formed are called **chemical changes**. Generally, although there are exceptions, these changes cannot be reversed: china cannot be turned back into clay. These changes are called chemical reactions. The chemical changes met so far in this section will happen whether air is present or not. The next section deals with chemical reactions in which one of the gases in air, oxygen, is vital.

BURNING

Children can be confused about the difference between heating and burning. When you heat a piece of paper strongly it will char, that is, slowly turn into a black mass of carbon. This will happen whether air is present or not. It is a chemical reaction in which one substance, paper, breaks down into simpler substances including carbon.

The reaction that takes place when you set fire to a piece of paper is different. This will happen only when air is present, because the paper reacts with one of the gases in air: oxygen.

Air is a mixture of gases, the main two being nitrogen (79%) and oxygen (20%). Nitrogen does not react easily, but oxygen will react chemically with many substances, especially at high temperatures.

Paper, wood, coal and oil can all be set alight: they are fuels. They all contain carbon and hydrogen. Once set alight the carbon in a fuel is able to join with oxygen from the air to make a new substance, the gas carbon dioxide. The hydrogen from the fuel joins oxygen from the air to make water vapour. At the same time energy is given out in the form of heat and light so that a flame, or at least a red glow, is seen.

To summarise: burning is a chemical reaction involving oxygen from the air. So, when someone says they have burned the toast, that is usually, except in extreme cases, a misuse of the word.

THE WATER CYCLE

'Where does all this rain come from? There can't be much left up there.' Would that it were so sometimes! Rain is part of a reversible physical process in which water turns to water vapour, and back again to water.

Water evaporates from the seas and oceans, particularly when heated by the Sun. The warm, moist air rises, and as it rises it cools. Cold air cannot contain as much water vapour as warm air, so some of the water condenses out as mist or cloud. Further cooling may bring the droplets of mist together into big drops which then fall as rain. The water runs into or over the ground and eventually into rivers which return it to the seas and oceans. So the water is returned to its source: it is continuously recycled (see Figure 6.3).

DISSOLVING

If you put a spoonful of sugar or salt into a glass of water and stir it, the sugar or salt will apparently disappear, leaving the water looking as clear as before. If you put a spoonful of powdered chalk into a glass of water and stir it, the mixture will look white and not clear. The chalk has not dissolved, but is

Figure 6.3

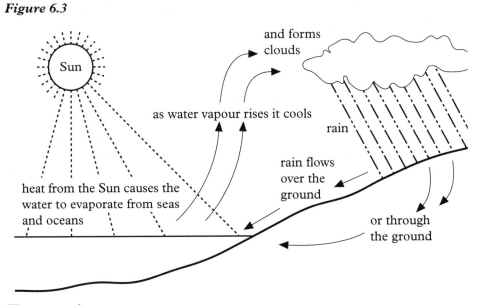

The water cycle

suspended in the water as a solid. In time it will all sink to the bottom of the glass.

The sugar is said to be **soluble**, and the chalk **insoluble**. The sugar gives a clear **solution** in water; the chalk gives a cloudy **suspension**. ('Clear' does not mean the same as colourless: orangeade may be coloured, but if you can see through the glass, it is clear, and therefore a solution.)

The sugar has separated out into very small particles, invisible even with a microscope. (The particles in a solution can be either molecules or ions, a distinction which does not become important until a later stage.)

Substances like sugar and salt which dissolve in water are said to be soluble, but this does not mean that if you add them indefinitely they will keep dissolving. Eventually a point is reached where no further salt or sugar will dissolve: the solution is then said to be **saturated**. The limit of how much you can dissolve is different for different substances. For example, if you measure out 100 cm^3 of water, you will be able to dissolve in it no more than 36 g of salt.

The figure is different for different substances: 100 cm^3 of water can dissolve 57 grams of washing soda crystals, or 204 grams of sugar. (These figures are for water at room temperature: it may be possible to dissolve more in hot water.)

In practice these figures are difficult to obtain quickly with any accuracy:

if you stir 36 g of salt into 100 g of water, most of it will dissolve fairly quickly, but it can take hours before the last few grains dissolve.

SEPARATING MIXTURES

We turn on the tap and expect the water coming out to be pure. If it comes out muddy we ring the water company. So it is with many other products we buy, like sugar and salt: they occur in nature as dirty mixtures, but we expect to buy them as pure substances.

Some of the ways in which we can separate mixtures of two or more substances, and so produce pure substances are by:

- sieving;
- filtration;
- evaporation.

Sieving

A gardener who is planting a new lawn will need the top layer of soil to be free from stones. He or she will need a sieve to shake the soil through, leaving the stones behind.

Soils can be investigated using a series of sieves with holes of different sizes. The particles will pass through sieves of decreasing mesh size, until they reach a mesh size too small to pass through. In this way the investigator can find out the proportion of each size of particle in the soil.

Filtration

The water companies separate mud and other solid matter from the water by passing the water through beds of sand called filter beds. This traps all the solids and lets clear water flow through. (Notice that clear water need not be pure water. There may still be substances dissolved in it, or solid substances, like bacteria, that are too small to filter out.)

An easy way to do the same in a classroom is by filtering the dirty water through filter paper placed in a funnel. If filter paper is not available, kitchen paper, newspaper or a lump of cotton wool will do. Newspaper is slow but efficient (although the ink can discolour the water); kitchen paper and cotton wool are faster but the water going through is likely to be cloudy.

The same method can be used to separate a mixture of two substances where only one of them will dissolve in water. Such mixtures could be sugar and chalk, or salt and sand. The mixture needs to be stirred with plenty of water until one has dissolved. You then filter the mixture: the chalk or sand will stay in the funnel, and the sugar or salt, dissolved in water, will pass through. If the sugar or salt solution is heated gently, the water will evaporate, leaving small crystals of sugar or salt.

Rock salt is purified in this way. Rock salt looks dirty and contains sand and other impurities. Dissolving and filtering remove these, and then the water has to be boiled away to give pure colourless salt.

The filter paper, or whatever is being used, is acting like a very fine sieve: it contains very small holes which allow the very small molecules of water through, but not the much larger particles of dirt or sand.

Evaporation

This is the method described above for removing the water from a dissolved substance. If a substance dissolves in water to form a clear liquid (called a solution) then it cannot be filtered out. You can see through a solution, even though the dissolved substance may have coloured it. The substance can only be extracted by boiling or evaporating the water away.

In hot countries, such as Southern France, sea water is run into shallow tanks where the heat of the sun will evaporate the water, leaving salt behind.

*S*UMMARY

- We are surrounded by all sorts of materials which children can investigate: some occur naturally and others are manufactured.
- Many of their properties involve looking and handling: others involve investigating with magnets or electrical circuits.
- Materials exists in three states: solid, liquid and gas.
- Materials can change from one state to another, unless heating decomposes them. This change of state is a physical process, and can be reversed. So water can be placed in a freezer to give ice, and the ice can be melted back into water. Any substance contains the same particles whichever state it is in, but arranged in a different way in each state.
- When substances are changed into different substances this is a chemical

change. Usually this cannot easily be reversed. Baking a cake is one example: a cake cannot be changed back into its ingredients.

● Burning (or combustion) is an example of a chemical reaction: it involves combining substances with oxygen from the air to form new substances.

● Many substances can be dissolved in water or other liquids to form solutions. There is a limit to the amount of a substance that can be dissolved in a given volume of water.

● Most substances do not occur as pure chemicals, but as mixtures of many other substances. There are many ways of separating mixtures: three of the simplest are sieving, filtration and evaporation.

● The ideas in this chapter on the properties of materials and the ways in which they can change will eventually lead to ideas about atoms and molecules, and the ways in which they determine the whole structure of the world.

7

Natural Materials

The Story of Rock

CARRIE BRANIGAN

Introduction   96
Grouping and classifying rocks   97
How rocks are formed   100
Uses of rocks   102
Summary   104

7

Natural Materials

THE STORY OF ROCK

CARRIE BRANIGAN

INTRODUCTION

Natural materials and the development of planet Earth are included within the subject of Earth science. It includes disciplines such as geology, meteorology, astronomy and hydrology and overlaps with geography and environmental studies. This chapter is about geology in that it describes how the Earth's natural materials are classified, formed and used.

By examining the geological evidence around us (i.e. rocks, soils and landscapes) we gain an understanding of the way in which the Earth is developing over millions of years. Not only is this study interesting, but all our everyday items originate from materials that make up the Earth; more obvious examples are bricks and clay pots.

The National Curriculum advocates using the child's own environment as a starting point for the development of knowledge and understanding of more general concepts associated with a study of the Earth. Most localities have usable samples of soil and possibly rock for investigation; buildings and constructions of stone or brick, and the effects of the weather on them, can provide useful sources of information leading to further study.

The areas of knowledge identified in the National Curriculum relate to different types of natural materials, their classification, their formation and their uses, and those suggested for study are rocks, soils and sands. Note that air and water are themselves defined as natural materials; it is their action in the formation and erosion of natural materials that is important to Earth science. The effects of water and air have a major role in the shaping of the landscapes we see around us.

GROUPING AND CLASSIFYING ROCKS

Familiar examples of rocks are limestone, clay, sandstone, slate, marble, basalt and granite. They appear to be very different from one another and may be found in very different locations. A definition of the term 'rock' is useful in understanding these natural materials, and one commonly used is:

> Any accumulation of minerals, whether consolidated (stuck
> together) or not, which forms part of the Earth's crust.

Therefore, limestone, clay, sandstone, slate, marble, basalt and granite are all rocks although they appear and feel very different from one another due to their mineral make-up. The term 'mineral' requires further explanation, and although this term is commonly used, e.g. mineral water, it does have a more specific definition:

> A mineral is a naturally occurring substance with a fixed chemical
> composition; it may occur as a crystal, depending on how it has
> been formed.

For example, the mineral quartz is a naturally occurring substance made of silicon and oxygen and often occurs as a crystal. Children may be familiar with its glassy appearance and needle-like crystal shape; amethyst is a purple variety of quartz that has been coloured by impurities when it was being formed. Quartz is found consolidated with other minerals in the rock granite and is also the main constituent of sand. Sand has usually been formed from the breakdown of rocks, such as granite, and the fine particles transported and dumped, for example, on beaches and river beds. The process of rocks breaking down to finer particles is part of the important recycling process that occurs on the Earth's surface. This will be further explained on p. 102.

The knowledge that rocks are made up of minerals leads us to some understanding of why rocks appear very different from one another. The common misconception that all rocks are large and grey can therefore be challenged. By collecting rocks from a variety of sources, their differences and similarities can be noted and rocks grouped together on this basis. However, the accurate classification of rocks can be a little more problematic. Each rock, such as granite, has a particular mineral make-up. Granites are not all the same because certain mineral types may be of a different colour or shape, as we have already seen with the example of quartz. When geologists classify rocks, they need to know not only what minerals the rock contains but also where the rock has come from. To complicate things further, the true identity of the rock may only be discovered by placing a thin section of it under a hand lens.

In general, there are particular features of rocks that can help us to classify them into broad groups. These groups are sedimentary, igneous and metamorphic; their names are derived from the way they have been formed. This is explained further on pp. 100–2.

Sedimentary rocks tend to be grainy in texture and familiar examples are sandstone and limestone. Sandstone, as the name implies, is made from grains of sand cemented together. Limestones, on the other hand, are formed in a variety of ways but the mineral calcium carbonate occurs in all types. Many sedimentary rocks contain fossils which are useful for interpreting the environment that existed during the formation of these rocks. A sedimentary rock under a microscope may look like Figure 7.1.

Figure 7.1

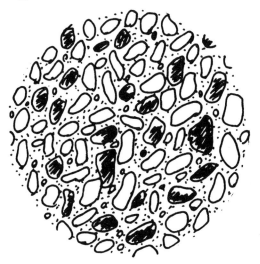

A sedimentary rock under a powerful hand lens, showing cemented grains (minerals)

Igneous rocks tend to have interlocking grains, giving the rock a crystalline appearance. Familiar examples are granite and basalt and under a microscope or hand lens may look like Figure 7.2.

Metamorphic rocks tend to have minerals that are lined up with a crystalline appearance. Familiar examples are slate and marble and under the microscope or hand lens may look like Figure 7.3.

Figure 7.2

An igneous rock under a powerful hand lens, showing the interlocking minerals

Figure 7.3

A metamorphic rock under a powerful hand lens, showing the minerals lined up

The physical characteristics, such as texture, colour, hardness, mineral size and shape, are the most obvious things to refer to when grouping rocks. The knowledge that sedimentary, igneous and metamorphic rocks have observable differences between them can help us to classify the rocks into these groups. Many classification keys have been produced and these may help as a focus for any such sorting. However, it is as well to remember the geologist's difficulties in the completion of the classification, and the naming, of rocks.

Other important issues in grouping and classifying natural materials refer to the common names and everyday materials we see around us. For example:

- gemstones and crystals are the common names used for the appearance of some minerals such as quartz and diamond;
- stones and pebbles are all rocks but are given these names because of their size and shape: stones are usually fragments of rock found in soil and may give some clue to the rocks nearby or underlying the location where they have been found; pebbles can be formed from any rock-type and become smoothed by the action of water;
- soil is the accumulation of loose, weathered material which covers much of the Earth's land-surface. It contains minerals and rock particles of varying size, plant material and products of the action of other living organisms. Soils can have very different textures and colours throughout the country such as the distinctive red soils in Devon which have originated from the underlying red sandstones.

HOW ROCKS ARE FORMED

As we briefly explained (pp. 98–9), rocks are classified as sedimentary, igneous and metamorphic according to the way they have been formed; 'sedimentary' and 'igneous' are terms that come from the Latin words *sedere* (to sit) and *ignis* (fire); the term 'metamorphic' comes from the Greek words *meta* (change) and *morphe* (form).

Sedimentary rocks

Sedimentary rocks are formed from the fragments of other rocks that have been weathered, eroded and then transported, by water, ice or wind, and finally deposited (settled) as sediments in water or dunes. Sedimentary rocks are being formed today. River and stream currents transport rock fragments; larger fragments roll along the river or stream bed while smaller fragments are carried by the current. These rock pieces are eventually dumped as sediment by slower-moving stretches of water when the current cannot move them any further. The sediments accumulate as layers of sand, mud and pebbles as the transportation process sorts the fragments by size. Their eventual alteration to rocks, by being compacted and cemented over millions of years, may allow the sediments to retain distinctive features of their formation, for example ripple marks that were once on the sea-bed. This means that these sedimentary rocks can be 'read' as a record of past conditions.

Igneous rocks

Igneous rocks are formed by the solidification of molten rock (the 'fire') or magma that originates deep in the Earth. Movements of this magma cause it to rise and cool and so eventually solidify. If this molten rock reaches the surface it flows out, as lava, to form volcanoes, and solidifies on the Earth's surface. Magma that does not reach the surface may cool deep within the Earth's crust and later become exposed at the Earth's surface by movements of the Earth, weathering and erosion. The minerals and their crystal size tell us how quickly or how slowly the magma and lava has cooled. The rock appearance is usually one of interlocking crystals, as described on page 98; the slower the magma or lava cooled, the bigger the crystals. Granite has large crystals; it cooled slowly deep within the Earth's crust. Basalt has small crystals; it cooled quickly on the Earth's surface as a result of volcanic activity. If the lava cooled very rapidly, for example in water, the rock may appear glassy as the separate minerals may have become fused together (as in the rock pitchstone, which looks like dark glass). A familiar igneous rock is pumice which has formed from froth emitted from particular types of volcanoes.

Metamorphic rocks

Metamorphic rocks result from the recrystallisation (change of form) of existing rocks and are formed by the action of heat and/or pressure. For example, a mass of magma that rises into the Earth's crust will cause a chemical change in the surrounding rocks; limestones alter to marble (used in ornamentation) and shales to slate (used in roofing), depending on the actual temperatures and pressures involved. The minerals will realign themselves or be replaced by new minerals, giving the rock a new crystalline texture, possibly banded, as in the rock gneiss (pronounced 'nice').

The oldest rocks (about 3,900 million years old), found in Greenland, are metamorphic, which implies that they were formed from even older rocks. As an example to illustrate the three rock-types occurring together 'in the field', we can use the granite masses of Devon and Cornwall. These were originally magma bodies (igneous) that rose into the Earth's crust. The surrounding rocks with which the magma came into contact were shales (sedimentary); because of the great heat on contact they were changed to slates (metamorphic) approximately 300 million years ago. The scenery that can be described today has resulted from the processes involved in weathering and erosion over this time span.

Although the rocks are classified into the three main groups according to the different processes involved in their formation, there are connections between the ways in which sedimentary, igneous and metamorphic rocks have been formed. These are represented in Figure 7.4, a diagram of the rock cycle which demonstrates the recycling nature mentioned on page 97.

THE USES OF ROCKS

Many natural materials are extracted from the Earth for manufacturing and building purposes and as energy resources. Such materials include sand, gravel, metals (from ores), oil and coal. Some building materials are used directly in their natural state (for example, slate) while others are fashioned and used as building stones or as decorative structures (for example, Bath stone and marble). A visit to a graveyard can reveal a variety of rock types used for the gravestones which usually occur locally. Some rocks may have been transported great distances, such as the stone used for St Paul's Cathedral; the white limestone originated from Portland, Dorset, over 100 miles away.

Investigating building materials can be used as a helpful analogy to natural Earth processes. Bricks are made by firing clay at high temperatures. This can be seen as a process similar to the formation of metamorphic rocks in which the minerals become permanently changed through the action of heat and pressure. Concrete can have similarities with certain sedimentary rocks, the fragments of which become 'glued' together by a cement.

The burning of fossil fuels, such as coal, oil and gas, provides a large amount of our energy requirements. These energy resources have been produced over millions of years from the remains of plants and animals: hence the term 'fossil fuel'. Coal has been formed from fossil plants that grew in swampy regions. It is graded for use today by its depth of burial during formation. Coal found at deeper levels contains more carbon (anthracite is 95% carbon) which gives the coal a higher heat-producing quality. Oil was

Figure 7.4

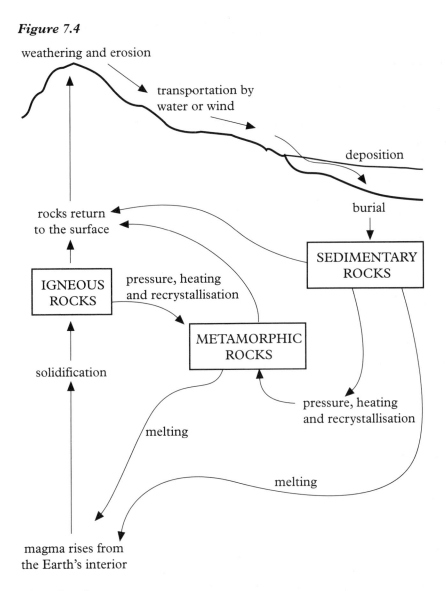

weathering and erosion

transportation by
water or wind

deposition

burial

rocks return
to the surface

SEDIMENTARY
ROCKS

IGNEOUS
ROCKS

pressure, heating
and recrystallisation

METAMORPHIC
ROCKS

solidification

pressure, heating
and recrystallisation

melting

melting

magma rises from
the Earth's interior

The rock cycle

formed in a different way. The remains of small marine organisms were deposited and compacted in an oxygen-free environment on the sea-bed. Further compaction causes the oil to seep out of these original rocks and migrate upwards through the layers of rock to collect in porous, reservoir rocks. Sometimes the oil may escape to the surface. Other resources that have similarities with the chemical nature of oil are natural gas, petroleum and tar.

All materials have their origins in the Earth. For example, plastic is made from oil; aluminium is extracted from the rock bauxite. However, the Earth's natural resources are finite and ways of conserving them have to be taken seriously, such as lessening our demand for them and recycling used materials. There are obvious connections here with environmental education and global awareness.

SUMMARY

- Through a study of rocks an interpretation of the geological history of our planet can be made.
- Rocks can be classified by their type of formation and can be seen to relate to one another in a recycling process described by the rock cycle.
- A very important aspect of any study of the Earth is that all of our everyday items can be manufactured from materials extracted from the Earth's crust.

8

Electricity

LINDA WEBB

Introduction   106

Uses of electricity   106

Safety   106

Mains electricity   107

What electricity is   108

Circuit components and their effects   114

Circuit drawings and diagrams   118

Summary   125

8

ELECTRICITY

LINDA WEBB

INTRODUCTION

For many people the word 'electricity' is associated with danger! The SPACE report on electricity (1991) shows that although children know how important electricity is in everyday life it is still associated with shocks and fire. Another problem is that electricity is invisible and so it is difficult to make sense of what is going on in the wires; thus a child's comment that 'Electricity is like magic' would ring true with many adults. In addition there are many words associated with electricity, such as 'power', 'voltage', 'amps' and 'current', which are difficult to understand (and which are quite often used incorrectly in the everyday world). In this chapter the aim is to give a basic outline of the words and ideas used in electricity.

USES OF ELECTRICITY

Even before they arrive in school, children will be aware that many objects need to be 'plugged in' or need batteries to make them work. They are, perhaps, not so aware that the 'magic' ingredient that makes these things work is **electricity**. Appliances that use electricity can be put into groups that do similar things, e.g. light bulbs and televisions give out **light**; radios, televisions and CD players give out **sound**; fires and immersion heaters provide **heat**; whilst the **movement** effect is put to good use in food mixers, washing machines and Scalextric.

SAFETY

Misuse of electricity can lead to electric shocks, burns and death.

In the classroom

It is important that pupils do not poke *anything* into the holes of an electric socket. All items that are used on the mains supply in school should be regularly checked for insulation by a registered contractor; if this is done they are usually safe to use. However, children should never be allowed to touch exposed metal parts of mains appliances. Batteries used in most games and toys are normally quite safe if touched, but if they are **short-circuited** (see page 110) they can cause the connecting wires to get very hot and may cause burning.

In the home

The same rules apply to sockets and batteries at home, but there are some other special safety points to be aware of. If a mains appliance breaks down, for instance, it is likely that the fuse will blow. The fuse is an important safety feature, and after repairing the appliance a fuse with the correct rating should be put back in the plug, *not any old wire or a piece of silver paper*. For example, an electric fire requires a 13 A fuse whereas a standard lamp needs only a 2 A fuse: the information about the correct fuse to use is normally supplied when you buy a new appliance. Sockets and any appliance connected to the mains should not be touched with wet hands. Because of the damp atmosphere in bathrooms a pull-cord is used to switch on the lights.

A further word of warning: cables which carry electricity on overhead pylons (including those for electric trains) and the ground-level track for underground trains can cause death on contact. **On no account should children go anywhere near them!**

MAINS ELECTRICITY

The major difference between mains electricity and that supplied by batteries is the voltage each provides. For instance, a typical battery supplies 6 volts but mains supplies 240 volts. With more volts more current can be sent through an object. The mains could send 40 times more electric current through a human body than a battery could, and it is partly the size of the current that causes the damage.

WHAT ELECTRICITY IS

In order to make sense of electricity we really need to understand a bit about what it is, and in order to do that we need to have some idea of what things are made of. Imagine a very powerful microscope looking into a piece of metal wire. You would see something like Figure 8.1: large solid 'lumps' of matter held together in a regular pattern by strong forces, with tiny particles wandering around in all directions between them. These tiny particles are called **electrons** and they have what we call 'negative' charge.

Figure 8.1

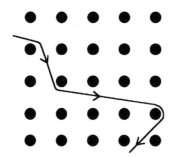

Movement of an electron as it moves through a solid
Note: On average the electron may pass about 100
atom cores before it suffers a significant deflection

Current

If a suitable force is applied by using a battery, the electrons in a metal wire can be persuaded to move along in a particular direction as shown in Figure 8.2(b).

Figure 8.2

(a)

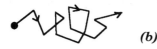

(b)

Electron movement
(a) Electron movement over a longer period than in
Figure 8.1
(b) Movement of an electron through a solid when
a voltage is applied

When the electrons move along in a certain direction the result is called an electric **current**. Typically the electrons 'drift' along at very low speeds, only a few millimetres per second. If you connect a lamp to a battery with wires about a metre long, an electron starting from one end of the battery would only just reach the other end before the battery 'dies'. (You may wonder why a light bulb comes on immediately you turn the switch on when the bulb may be metres away from the switch. In fact, a signal is instantaneously sent along the wire telling all the individual electrons to start moving. Because this signal travels so fast, over the relatively short distances we experience, all the electrons appear to move off at the same time).

The size of a current is measured in amperes, or amps, which is usually abbreviated to A. That is, a current of two amps is written as 2 A. This flow of electrons is the same all the way around the circuit, which also means that the current is the same all the way around the circuit. Many people are not happy with this idea because they 'feel' that components in a circuit must use something up. In fact what happens is that electrical energy is converted to other forms (such as heat) and so might seem to be 'used up', but electric current is *not*.

Conductors and insulators

Materials that allow electricity to pass through them easily are called **good conductors** of electricity. All of the metals and one non-metal, carbon, are good conductors. This is because they contain a large number of electrons that are free to move around between the fixed parts of the atoms.

There are some materials, especially plastics, that have no electrons free to move about; these do not conduct electricity and are called **insulators**. There are also some materials which contain some electrons which are free to move about (but not as many as in the metals) and these are called **semi-conductors**. This group contains silicon and germanium.

Incomplete circuits

Air is a very poor conductor of electricity. Only if the voltage is great enough relative to the size of the gap will sparks be produced. With the low voltages used in schools, any air gap, for example a break in the circuit or a loose connection, will prevent any current from flowing. So check all around the circuit if there seems to be nothing happening.

Short circuits

In any circuit, if you connect a wire in parallel with any component you would 'short out' that component. Electricity is able to pass through the wire more easily than through the component, so only a little current will pass through the component and it might not work. This is particularly serious if you connect a wire across the ends of a battery. This is called a 'short circuit'. Because the wire has such a low resistance the battery is able to pass a very large current . This will probably make the wire very hot and will cause the battery to run down extremely quickly.

Complete circuits

In order to make electrical components or appliances work, electric current has to flow through them. To make the electrons flow the two ends of a battery (or the live and neutral wires of the mains supply) have to be joined to the component. In other words a complete loop, or **circuit,** has to be made (see Figure 8.3).

Figure 8.3

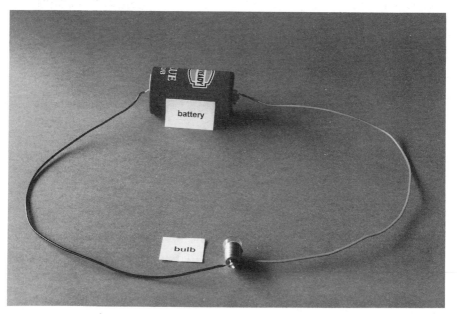

An electrical circuit

The light bulb can be made to light up by joining one end of the battery to the knob on the bottom of the bulb, and the other end to the 'screwy' part of the bulb. As soon as the circuit is complete a signal is sent almost instantaneously to all parts of the circuit. On receiving this signal all the electrons (in the wire connections, in the filament wire, in the metal 'screwy' bit and in the battery) in the circuit begin to move and a current flows. The bulb, like most other components, can let through electricity in either direction, so it doesn't matter which way round the bulb is connected.

If a buzzer were put in the circuit in place of the bulb it too would work (but be careful, some of them only work when placed one particular way round: if it doesn't work first time just disconnect it, then try the other way round).

Testing for conductors and insulators The circuit above can be modified slightly (Figure 8.4) to test different materials, to see if they are conductors or insulators: if the bulb lights up the test material is a conductor; if it does not (and the rest of the components are all working properly) it is an insulator.

Figure 8.4

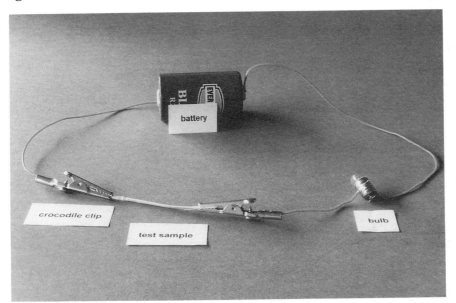

A circuit to test for conducting and insulating materials

Voltage

To gain a fuller understanding of these simple circuits and lay a foundation for understanding more complex circuits, we must look at the ideas of voltage (or potential difference) and resistance.

One of the simplest ways to think about voltage (or potential difference) is as the electrical force that pushes the electrons round the electric circuit. A large voltage makes the electrons move faster and therefore causes a larger current to flow. Voltage is also connected to the amount of power that can be delivered. A household light bulb, for example, is designed to be used with the 240 volt mains supply. A 1.5 volt torch battery cannot supply enough power to light it up; it needs more volts. So if the mains supply can supply more power than a 1.5 volt battery, just think how much more power over-head cables, at, say 33,000 volts could deliver! (The international abbreviation for the volt is V.)

Resistance

Not all materials behave in the same way when a voltage is connected across them; this is to do with the number of electrons inside the material that are free to move. Plastics, for example, have almost no 'free' electrons and even thousands of volts would produce no current. As we said on page 109, these materials are called insulators and are said to have a high **resistance**. Metals and carbon, however, contain a large number of electrons that are free to move, so relatively low voltages will produce a current. These are good conductors, so we say they have low resistance. Copper has particularly low resistance, and is therefore useful for making connecting leads (although these days copper is quite expensive and cheaper alloys are often used instead of pure copper).

When resistance is measured, the unit used is the ohm. The symbol for ohm is Ω. All components in a circuit have resistance, some more than others. The size of the resistance of a component stays the same, no matter how hard you try to push a current through it (unless it gets hot).

The relationship between current, voltage and resistance

As we saw on page 36, potential difference, or voltage, can be thought of as the 'push' needed to send an electric current through a resistor. If you want a larger current in a particular circuit you must push the electrons harder. You do that by using a larger voltage. By taking measurements, we find that if you want to double the current you must double the voltage. (This is a simple way of stating **Ohm's Law**.)

Resistance tells us how many volts are needed to send a particular current through a component. We compare the resistances of different components by finding out the size of the voltage that would be needed to send a current of 1 amp through each component. If, for instance, 12 volts are needed to send a current of 1 amp through a buzzer, we would say that the buzzer had a resistance of 12 'volts for every amp', or 12 ohms. Using the relationship described above, this would also mean that a current of 0.5 amps would be produced from 6 volts, and 24 volts would send 2 amps through the buzzer. Very simply, resistance can be calculated from this formula:

$$\text{resistance} = \frac{\text{voltage}}{\text{current}}$$

or

$$\text{ohms} = \frac{\text{volts}}{\text{amps}}$$

The following gives an idea of the resistances of some components that you might use:

- mains 60 W light bulb   960 Ω
- torch bulb   60 Ω
- small motor   50 Ω
- relay   80 Ω
- buzzer   240 Ω

For the mathematically minded, current in a circuit can also be calculated (by rearranging the formula above):

$$\text{current (in amps)} = \frac{\text{potential difference (in volts)}}{\text{resistance (in ohms)}}$$

Thus, if the number of batteries in a circuit increases (i.e. there is more voltage) and the resistance stays the same, the current will increase. Conversely, if the resistance in the circuit is increased (say, by increasing the number of bulbs) without increasing the number of batteries, the current will decrease.

CIRCUIT COMPONENTS AND THEIR EFFECTS

Cells and batteries

A **cell** is a device which can produce an electrical voltage; it can consist of two different metals put into an acid. (In the Science Museum in London a knife and fork stuck into a lemon make a cell that is used to drive a motor.) The dry 'battery' that we use in torches, clocks, and so on, is, in fact, a single cell. A series of cells joined end to end makes larger voltages, and is called a **battery**. A 9 volt battery is made of six 1.5 volt cells joined end to end. So strictly speaking, a 1.5 volt battery is not a battery at all! For the rest of this chapter, however, I shall stick to common usage and call all cells and batteries 'batteries'.

Resistors (fixed and variable)

A **resistor** is a component that can be put into a circuit, its main use (in these simple circuits) being to limit the size of the current. Resistors can be manufactured of carbon or wire, can be made to a fixed value, or be made to vary up to a fixed value. Figure 8.5 shows a carbon resistor which has a fixed value. Its 'body' is usually about a centimetre long and has coloured stripes at one end. These stripes tell you its resistance and the accuracy of that resistance. You will need a colour code to work out the values.

Figure 8.5

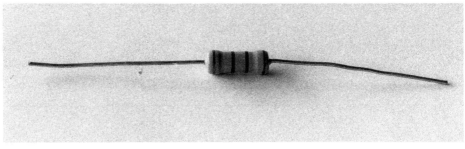

A resistor

A useful property of a wire (which is the same thickness all along) is that its resistance increases in proportion to its length, i.e. a wire that is 100 cm long has twice the resistance of an identical wire that is 50 cm long. Thus you could make high- and low-value resistors by using long or short lengths of wire.

A more exciting use, however, is to make a **variable resistor**. If you connect a length, say 100 cm, of a wire with high resistance into a circuit as shown in Figure 8.6, you could alter the resistance, and hence the current in the circuit. This would be shown by the brightness of the bulb. A long length of wire would have high resistance, giving a small current and a dim bulb. (Conversely, a short length of wire would have low resistance, give a large current and a bright bulb. The short wire might get hot!)

Figure 8.6

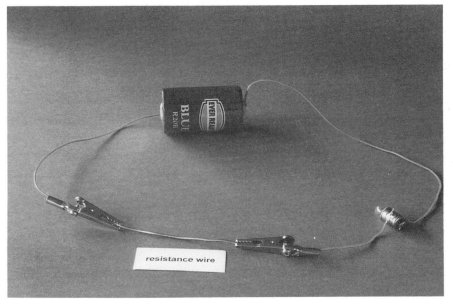

Altering the resistance of a circuit

You can buy variable resistors; in secondary schools you may find wire-wound **rheostats** and in an electronics shop or from a catalogue you could buy a much smaller one made from carbon, which is called a **potentiometer**. A potentiometer is shown in Figure 8.7.

Connecting wires

Connecting wires or **leads** in a circuit are usually made from copper or an alloy of copper. This is because it has a low resistance (and has little effect on the rest of the circuit). Wires may be made of lots of strands or they may be solid. Often they are surrounded by an insulating material, such as plastic or an enamel paint (which makes it look bright and shiny). Don't forget that the

Figure 8.7

A potentiometer

coating is an insulator, so should be stripped away from the copper at the end before joining it up to a component.

Lamps or bulbs

Despite their common use in simple circuits, many pupils do not really understand how light bulbs work. Figure 8.8 is a diagram of a light bulb. Notice that there are two connections (at the base and at the side of the bulb) to the filament of the bulb. Because of its high resistance, when current passes through the filament it gets so hot that it gives out light as well as heat. The bulb can carry electricity in either direction, so it doesn't matter which way round the bulb is connected.

Buzzers

Figure 8.9 shows what a typical buzzer looks like. Some only work in a particular voltage range (at too low a voltage – it doesn't work; at too high a voltage – it burns out!) and with the current in one particular direction. These are usually indicated on the buzzer. Contrary to what you may think, a larger current through the buzzer caused by using more batteries does not necessarily increase the loudness of the buzzer.

Figure 8.8

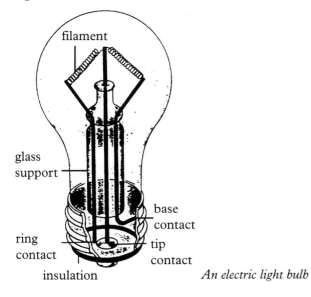

An electric light bulb

Figure 8.9

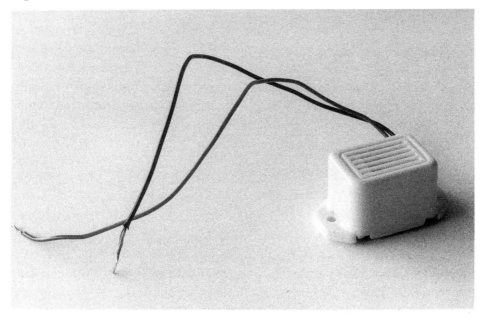

A buzzer

Motors

A typical motor is shown in Figure 8.10. This time, however, varying the current through it will change its speed, but again, too much current would cause it to burn out. Changing the direction of the current changes the direction of rotation of the motor.

Figure 8.10

An electric motor

Switches

It is useful to include at least one switch in any circuit that you make. A switch works by disconnecting or joining wires. A simple switch can leave the circuit permanently switched on or off, whilst a push switch leaves the circuit off and only switches the circuit on when it is held down. Examples of both are shown in Figure 8.11. Switches can be used to control electrical devices.

CIRCUIT DRAWINGS AND DIAGRAMS

Symbols

Electrical components can look quite complicated and, particularly for young children, are quite difficult to draw. To make life simpler there is an internationally accepted way to represent all electrical components and to show the circuits in which they are joined. The international symbols for components in common use are shown in Figure 8.12.

Figure 8.11

(a)

(b)

Switches
(a) A simple switch (b) A push switch

Figure 8.12

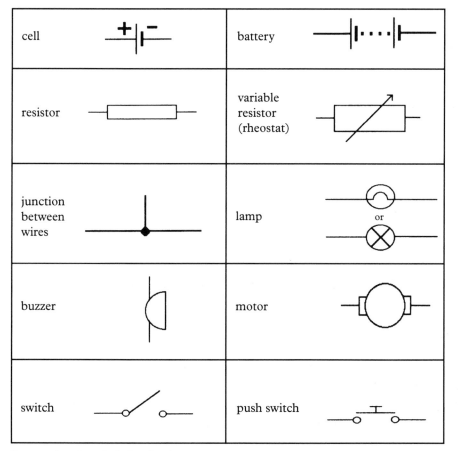

International symbols for circuit components

Connecting wire is shown as a straight line, even though in real life the wire may be anything but straight. It is helpful to keep the diagrams as neat as possible. However, children can experience real difficulty in translating a circuit diagram into a real circuit. Figure 8.13 shows some circuit diagrams drawn with the conventional symbols. Notice that there are no gaps in the circuit, apart from those between the lines representing the battery or batteries and the open switch.

Figure 8.13

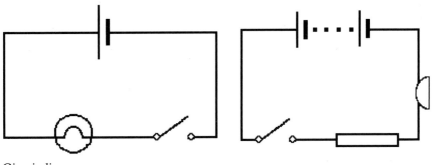

Circuit diagrams

Now that the symbols have been introduced, rather than describe the circuits, circuit diagrams are given.

More complex circuits

Series circuits When all the components in a circuit are joined in a line you have a series circuit. If you start with a simple circuit of one battery and one bulb you can easily add more batteries to the circuit. You will soon find that the direction in which the batteries are connected is important: adding more batteries in the same direction (joining + to –) increases the voltage and sends more current round the circuit, making the bulb shine brighter. If, however, you join the batteries so that + meets +, or – meets – then the voltage is decreased (possibly to zero), and the bulb is dimmer. Some examples are given in Figure 8.14.

Joining more components into a series circuit reduces the current (because each component has resistance), so any lamps in the circuit will be dimmer (or may not light up at all). As some components (e.g. a switch or a short length of copper wire) have only a very small resistance, their effect on the circuit may hardly be visible.

Figure 8.14

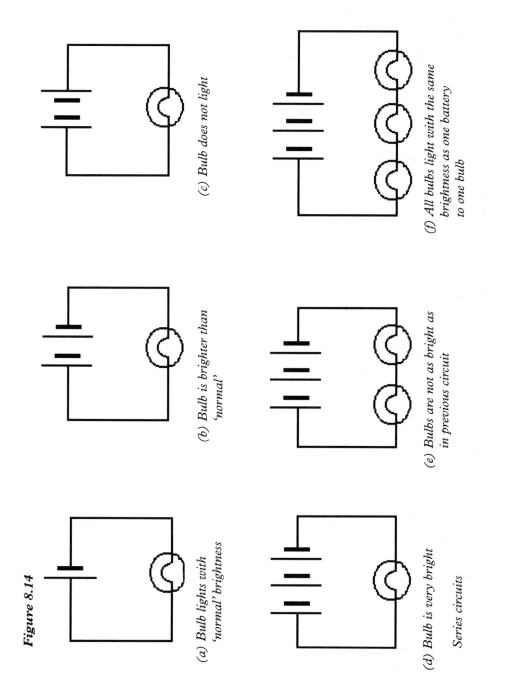

(a) Bulb lights with 'normal' brightness

(b) Bulb is brighter than 'normal'

(c) Bulb does not light

(d) Bulb is very bright

(e) Bulbs are not as bright as in previous circuit

(f) All bulbs light with the same brightness as one battery to one bulb

Series circuits

Parallel circuits A parallel circuit is different from a series one; instead of joining all the components up in a line, some components are connected across each other. Batteries joined in parallel are shown in Figure 8.15. This way of joining them is not used very often because it does not increase the voltage and therefore has little effect on the circuit.

Figure 8.15

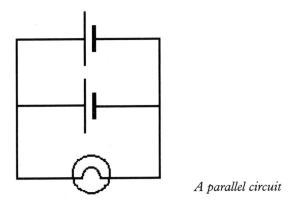

A parallel circuit

Three bulbs connected in parallel with each other and connected to a battery are shown in Figure 8.16. Each bulb should light up as if it alone were connected to the battery. Remove one bulb, and there is no effect on the others. This is, in fact, the way in which light bulbs are connected up at home, and if one bulb 'blows' the rest will remain alight.

Figure 8.16

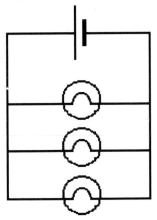

A parallel circuit with three bulbs

When components are connected in parallel the current divides up to go through the individual components. If all the components have the same resistance the current will split up evenly and equal currents will pass through each component. If, however, the components have different resistances a greater current will pass through the smaller resistance than through the larger ones. If you add up the currents passing through each of the components you will find that your result is equal to the total current going into (and coming out of) your components connected in parallel.

You can make some gloriously complicated circuits, as shown in Figure 8.17, with the results described there. Other components described earlier could, of course, be joined in circuits similar to those shown for the bulbs.

Figure 8.17

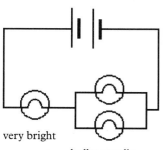

very bright

bulbs equally
bright but dimmer
than first bulb

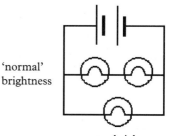

'normal'
brightness

extra bright

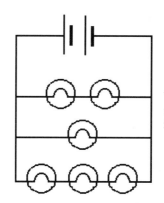

You will have to
try this circuit
for yourself!

More complicated circuits

Figure 8.18

(a) Light-
   dependent
   resistor

(b) Diode

(c) Thermistor

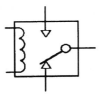

(d) Light-
   emitting
   diode

(e) Relay

(f) Voltmeter

(g) Ammeter

Some circuit components

Why the circuits may not work

Battery and bulb

1   The battery might be flat – see if it will light a bulb you know is not damaged.
2   The bulb might have 'blown' – see if a battery that you know works will light it.
3   The bulb might be the wrong voltage for the battery; a bulb rated at 2.5 V 0.3 A means that the bulb will run at normal brightness if connected to 2.5 volts. If it is connected to 1.5 volts it will be dimmer, while 4.5 volts or 6 volts will make it light very brightly and may cause it to 'blow'.
4   The connecting leads may be faulty – check that good connections have been made and that none of the wire's plastic cover is trapped in any of the connections. (The plastic is an insulator and will not allow current to pass through it.)
5   There may be a 'short circuit'.

Other components

Some components work only if they are connected the right way round (e.g. light-emitting diodes (LED), some buzzers). Components will not work if they are faulty: it's a good idea to check them before you use them in a complex circuit. You need only connect them to a battery with the correct voltage (written on the appliance or given in the manufacturer's information sheet) and see if they do what you would expect (for example, you should hear a slight 'click' when a relay is switched on or off).

Pictures and symbols for a number of components are shown in Figure 8.18.

SUMMARY

- When adequate care is taken it is safe to use mains electricity.
- Fuses of the correct rating must be used for all electrical appliances.
- Sockets and appliances connected to the mains supply should not be touched with wet hands.
- Children should not play near pylons or electrified ground level rail track.
- An electric current is a flow of particles called electrons.

- When the switch in a complete circuit is turned on, a signal is instantaneously sent through the whole circuit, so that electrons throughout the circuit start moving at the same time.
- The current is the same throughout a simple loop (non-branching) circuit. Currrent is not 'used up'.
- Electric current is measured in amps.
- Metals and carbon are good conductors of electricity. Poor electrical conductors (e.g. plastic, air) are called electrical insulators.
- An air gap in a circuit, or a faulty connection, will prevent electricity from flowing.
- Voltage can be considered as the electrical push on electrons.
- All electrical components resist the current to some extent.
- Resistance is measured in ohms.
- Electrical resistance can be calculated from the formula:

$$\text{resistance} = \frac{\text{voltage}}{\text{current}}$$

- There are many components which are designed for use in low-voltage circuits.
- Circuit diagrams are simplified by using standard symbols.
- A circuit in which there is more than one route (or loop) along which a current can pass is called a parallel circuit.
- Fault-finding in circuits should be done methodically.

Reference

J. Osborne, P. Black, M. Smith and J. Meadows, *Primary SPACE Project Research Report: Electricity*: Liverpool: Liverpool University Press, 1991.

9

Forces and Motion

JIM JARDINE AND JENNY
KENNEDY

Introduction	128
What is a force?	128
What can forces do?	130
Other forces	133
Forces on a motionless object	133
Weight	135
Floating and sinking	137
Forces always come in pairs	141
Falling objects – air resistance	142
Friction between solids	143
Keeping going	144
Speed	146
Summary	147

9

FORCES AND MOTION

JIM JARDINE
JENNY KENNEDY

INTRODUCTION

The meaning of the word 'force'

In general use, the word 'force' often conveys the idea of intense effort and even violence. But in science a force is simply a push or a pull, no matter how small. You exert a small force to blow a crumb from the table (a push), or to lift a spoon (a pull). If a broken-down car is to be shifted, you could exert a large push from behind, or get a breakdown truck to exert a large pull forward, or a crane to exert a large force upward to lift it on to the truck.

WHAT IS A FORCE?

All around us there are examples of forces being exerted. You provide forces when you push a bicycle along, pull a push-chair up a step, open a drawer, throw a ball, and so on. A force is a push or a pull. Notice that a force is needed to start something moving, although, as we shall see, a force may not be necessary to keep it moving.

In Figure 9.1 arrow-heads are used to show the directions of the forces mentioned and the places where they are applied, although there is nothing to indicate the relative sizes of those forces.

It is important to realise that in each of those examples there are also many other forces acting on the objects shown. In the case of the bike, in addition to the girl's push, there is the pull of gravity downward, which we call the bike's weight; the support of the ground pushing up on the bike; and the frictional forces of the road on the tyres and of the air pushing back on the whole bike (see Figure 9.2).

Figure 9.1

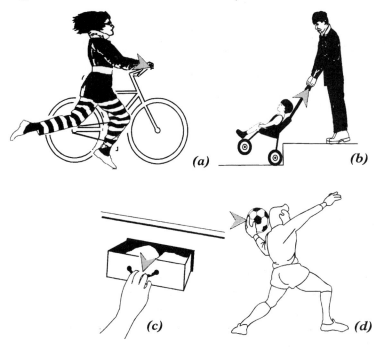

Forces which start things moving
(a) Pushing a bike
(b) Pulling a push-chair up a step
(c) Pulling a drawer open
(d) Throwing a ball

Notice that if we are interested in what happens to the bike, we concentrate on the forces acting *on* the bike. We ignore forces acting on other things. The bike's weight is pushing on the ground, perhaps making tyre-marks in the mud. The force of friction between the girl's shoes and the ground prevents her slipping, and so on. But we are not interested in the mud or the shoes. If you want to know what happens to an object when forces act on it, isolate the object in your mind and consider only the forces which push or pull that object. It is the combined effect of all the forces acting on an object which determines whether or not the object moves.

Figure 9.2

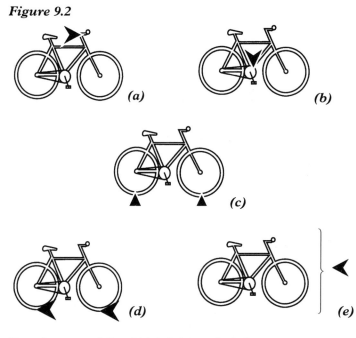

Some forces on a bike which is being pushed along
(a) Push on the bike: a forward force
(b) Pull of gravity (weight): a downward force
(c) Support of the ground: an upward force
(d) Friction between tyres and ground making wheels turn: a backward force
(e) Friction between air and bike: a backward force

WHAT CAN FORCES DO?

Alter the movement of an object

We again consider the movement of the bike, and concentrate on the effect of successively applying various single forces to it (see Figure 9.3).

From being stationary, if you push the bike forward it will start to move forward: push harder and the bike will go faster. Someone applying a force in the opposite direction can slow it down and eventually stop it. A force applied sideways can make the bike skid sideways, i.e. change its direction. Notice that in each of the five cases, a force has caused a change in the movement of the bike. The force has changed the bike's speed or the direction in which it is moving.

A force is needed to make an object start to move, to make it go faster,

Figure 9.3

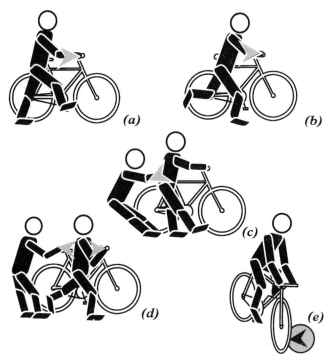

A force is needed to change the movement of a bike
(a) Starting off
(b) Speeding up
(c) Slowing down
(d) Stopped
(e) Changing direction

slow it down, stop it or make it change direction. In other words, a force is needed to change the movement of an object.

Change the shape of an object

It is possible for a single applied force to change the shape of an object. A ball is temporarily squashed by the force of the bat which hits it (Figure 9.4). However, since most balls are 'elastic', they recover their shape so quickly that we don't see the squashed shape, except by a special photographic technique. However, a ball of plasticine or of dough does retain its distorted shape. A large lump of plasticine hung on a string will be flattened by a whack with a bat or dented by a jab with a pencil. In each case, an applied force causes the lump to change its shape. If the lump of plasticine is on a surface, an additional force of friction with the surface comes into play.

When a pair of forces acts on an object, it can make the object twist, squash, stretch, break or tear, by moving one part of the object relative to another part (see Figure 9.4). All of these are examples where forces can cause one part of an object to move relative to another part of the same object. Forces can change the shape of an object.

Figure 9.4

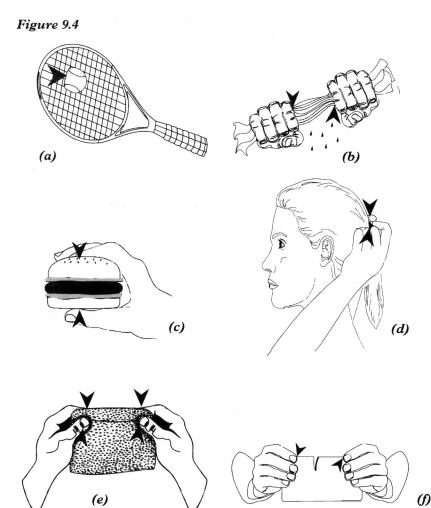

Forces can change the shape of an object
(a) Squashing a ball
(b) Twisting (wringing out) a dishcloth
(c) Squashing a roll
(d) Stretching a hairband
(e) Squeezing a sponge
(f) Tearing paper

OTHER FORCES

Electrostatic forces

So far we have concentrated on forces which are exerted by direct contact. It is possible, however, to exert forces 'at a distance' – that is, without any physical contact. You have probably combed your (clean) hair on a dry day and found that the comb then attracts strands of your hair without touching them. This is an electric force; or, since the electricity is not flowing as an electric current but is static, an 'electrostatic' force. Many plastic objects can be 'charged' by rubbing them on cloth or paper. As well as those forces which attract, it is also possible to produce electric forces which repel.

Magnetic forces

If you have played with magnets you will know that a magnet will pull a nearby piece of iron (or other magnetic material) towards itself. The Earth behaves like a huge magnet, and a compass is simply a small bar magnet which is free to turn around until it points in a north–south direction. We call the end of the magnet (or compass needle) which points to the north the 'north pole' of the magnet, and the other end the 'south pole'.

Using either two compass needles or two bar magnets you discover that the north pole of one attracts the south pole of the other. But two similar poles (i.e. two north poles or two south poles) push each other away – that is, they repel one another.

The force of gravity

There is a force we experience all the time which also acts through empty space. It is the Earth's gravitational pull and it differs from electric and magnetic forces in that there is no repulsive gravitational force. Gravity only pulls things together (see also section on weight, pages 135–6).

FORCES ON A MOTIONLESS OBJECT

A tug-of-war gives us a nice example of several forces all acting along the same line. Imagine that each member of both teams is equally strong and that we're not concerned with tactics. The pull, or force, that each member of the team exerts on the rope is then the same size, but of course the two teams pull in opposite directions along the rope.

Concentrate on the knot in the middle. With three people on each side, as as in Figure 9.5(a), there are three equal forces pulling each way – the knot stays still and it's a draw. No prizes for guessing which team in Figure 9.5(b) wins. The larger overall force to the left makes the knot move to the left. What happens when the teams go off for a break, as in Figure 9.5(c)? The knot stays still – with no forces pulling sideways in either direction. The rope remains on the ground because the ground produces an upward force to balance the rope's weight pushing down.

Figure 9.5

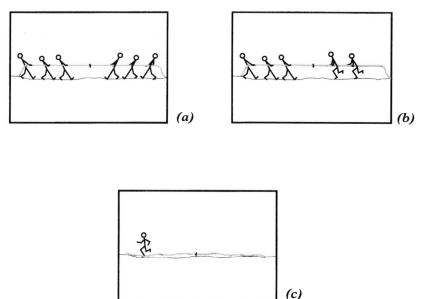

(a) *(b)* *(c)*

Forces in a tug-of-war

If you can imagine a stationary object with no forces at all acting on it (it would have to be beyond the range of any force due to gravity), that too would remain motionless.

So if an object is not moving, either the forces acting on the object in each direction balance out or there are no forces acting on the object at all.

WEIGHT

It is easy to think of examples of how we ourselves exert forces – by pushing and pulling – and not difficult to think of forces exerted by other animals: horses draw carts; a lioness cuffs a cub; a hawk lifts its prey. It is easy to find evidence that wind, rain and waves push on objects: branches of trees are blown around; you can hear rain battering the windows; waves knock down sandcastles.

But are there any forces acting on an object which is just sitting still: a jar of honey in the cupboard; a rucksack on your shoulder; a sleeping baby in a cot; a toy boat in a bath? And are they pushing or pulling, exerting forces on anything? Well, strange as it may seem, they are, although this is not at all obvious. As we have seen, everything on or near the Earth is pulled in towards the Earth's centre by an invisible force which we call gravity. The force of gravity on an object is known as the object's weight. The weights of the jar of honey, the rucksack, the baby, the toy boat, are all forces pulling them down. If these objects do not move there must be upward forces, equal to their weights, supporting them (see Figure 9.6).

Figure 9.6

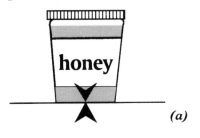

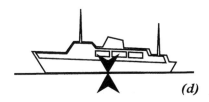

(a)

(b)

(c)

(d)

Balanced forces
(a) Honey jar
(b) Rucksack
(c) Baby on a mattress
(d) Toy boat floating

Gravity pulls the jar of honey down on the shelf (with no visible effect unless the shelf is flimsy). The shelf 'pushes up' to balance the weight. A rucksack on your back is pulling down on your shoulder (which you can feel, and others can see an effect if your shoulder sags). Your shoulder provides the upward push. A sleeping baby is pulled down on the cot mattress. The mattress, albeit squashed, pushes up. And as for the boat, its weight pulls it downward. The water pushes up to balance the boat's weight.

Now you know what we can say about the forces acting on a stationary object on Earth. The gravitational force downwards, the weight, is balanced by an upward force of the same size – provided in all our examples by the 'support': the shelf, your shoulders, the cot mattress, the water. (If there were any other forces acting on one of those objects but it remained still, the extra forces would also have to balance one another.) Note that atmospheric pressure does not feature in the above.

We can find how much something weighs, the force of gravity pulling it down, if we let a forcemeter (sometimes called a 'spring balance') support it. A bag of fruit could be hung on a forcemeter so that it isn't falling or bouncing or moving in any other way. The downward force, the weight of fruit, must then be balanced by the upward force of the forcemeter, and the weight of the fruit is shown on the forcemeter. The scale on the forcemeter is marked off in newtons, N for short. A medium-sized apple weighs about 1 newton.

The distinction between the two concepts **mass** and **weight** is often troublesome. The mass of an object is a measure of how much material (atoms and molecules) there is making up the object. The more 'stuff' there is, the more difficult it is to slow an object down or to accelerate it. So its mass is also a measure of the object's 'reluctance to move' or its 'inertia'. Think of the comparison between starting off in a car, first laden with the family and holiday baggage, and then in the empty car. The car with more 'stuff' in it – more mass – finds it harder to accelerate. Mass is measured in grams (g) or kilograms (kg).

Mass and weight are related. Weight is the force of gravity pulling an object to the centre of the Earth. The more mass which comprises an object the more 'stuff' there is to be pulled downwards. In fact, mass and weight are directly proportional. Double the mass and the weight doubles.

The Moon's gravity is less than the Earth's, so objects, including people, become lighter on the Moon. However, they are still made of as much stuff as when they were on Earth, so they still have the same mass. In 'outer space', well away from any planet or star, everything becomes absolutely weightless.

FLOATING AND SINKING

Floating

Why do some objects float and others sink? The answer is not as easy as 'heavy things sink; light things float', nor 'small things float; large things sink', as a lot of children say, even after investigations into what will or won't float. Huge oil tankers weighing several thousand million newtons float, while small pebbles, weighing perhaps a quarter of a newton, sink. In the following explanation of floating and sinking, consider the objects as placed on the surface of calm water. Hurling the ball or a turbulent water surface would introduce complications.

Think of a beach-ball floating on calm water. Notice in Figure 9.7(a) that the ball does not sit right on the surface of the water. If the beach-ball is still, the forces on it must be balanced. The weight of the beach-ball is acting downward. The water must be providing a force upward. We call this force the 'upthrust' – 'thrust' being another word for 'force'.

If, however, you start by supporting the ball so that part of it is just below the water surface (Figure 9.7(b)), it will sink a bit when you take your hand away. In this case, there was at the start some upthrust of the water but it wasn't enough to balance the weight of the ball.

If you try slowly pushing a beach-ball down into a basin of water you can feel that there is an upward force which is pushing against you. (Figure 9.7(c)). This upthrust increases as more and more of the ball is pushed below the water surface. If you have to push down to keep the ball under water, it will shoot up when you take your hand away. The upthrust must have been too big to balance the weight of the ball.

You can see from the diagrams that if only a small bit of the ball is under water you don't get enough upthrust to keep it afloat. If too much of the ball is under water, the upthrust is too great. When the ball is floating on its own, the upthrust is just enough to balance the weight of the ball.

An object, such as the beach-ball, placed on water, sinks further and further into the water until the upthrust is exactly equal to the weight of the object. It is then floating, with the forces balanced.

If you repeat this experiment with a house brick, the upthrust will never be as big as the weight of the brick no matter how far it sinks into the water. The brick will therefore never float. It sinks to the bottom of the water.

What then determines how big the water's upthrust on any particular object will be? To answer this consider the following. Imagine floating a beach-ball in a basin which is already full to the brim with water. Some of the

Figure 9.7

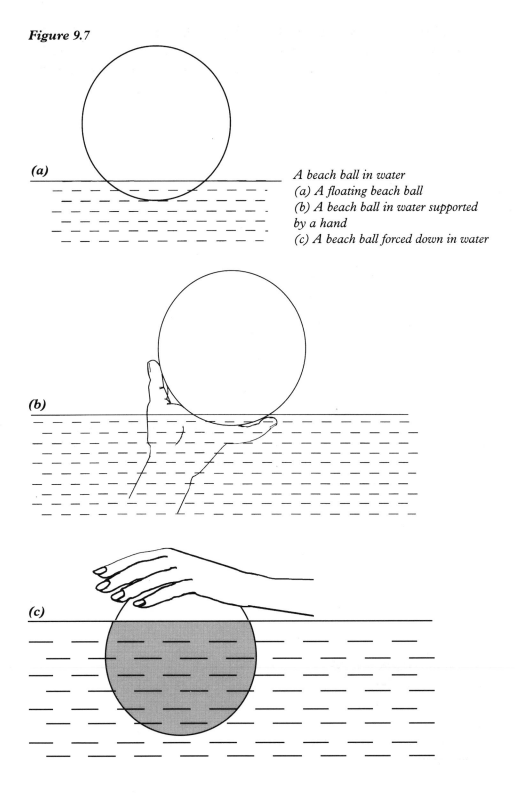

A beach ball in water
(a) A floating beach ball
(b) A beach ball in water supported by a hand
(c) A beach ball forced down in water

water will spill over (be 'displaced'; see Figure 9.8). It turns out that the weight of this displaced water is the same as the weight of the whole beach-ball. So if something is floating it is displacing its own weight of water. How can we explain this?

Figure 9.8

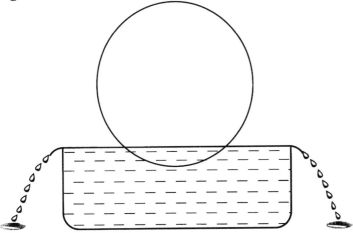

A beach ball displaces water

In Figure 9.9 the arrow-head shows the direction of the upthrust (not the size of the force, nor the direction of any movement). Remember that there is also a force acting downwards, the beach-ball's weight.

Figure 9.9

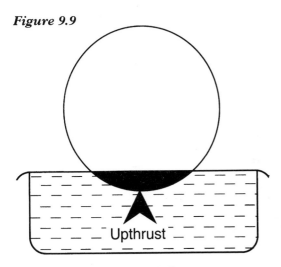

Upthrust supports a beach ball

When the ball is floating, the force pushing it up (upthrust) must be the same size as the force which supported the displaced water before it spilled over, since that upthrust had kept the water which was subsequently displaced in position. Also the displaced water took up the same volume as the shaded portion of the ball in Figure 9.9. As this upthrust held that shaded bit of water up, it must be equal to the weight of that bit of water: that is, to the weight of the water displaced.

The size of the upthrust equals that of the weight of water displaced: also the upthrust is equal to the weight of the floating ball – balanced forces.

So, to summarise the theory of floating:

upthrust = weight of water displaced

and

upthrust = weight of floating ball

and so,

weight of water displaced = weight of floating ball.

In other words, the floating ball displaces its own weight of water.

Sinking

The only thing that determines whether or not an object will float when gently placed on calm water is whether or not it can displace its own weight of water. A solid plasticine ball will sink, but if it is made into the shape of a boat it might float. In the first case it cannot displace its own weight of water. In the second case it can.

Consider a solid plasticine lump the same size and shape as the beach-ball. If placed on water it would sink, displacing (pushing out of the way) more and more water as it 'went under'. Once it is completely immersed, it can displace no more water, but it continues to sink. The force pushing up on the lump is the upthrust of the water on it. Because the beach-ball and the lump are identical in volume, they each displace the same volume of water: the upward force, the upthrust, is the same on the lump as on the fully immersed ball. The force downward on the lump is its weight. For the lump, this upthrust is not great enough to balance the lump's large weight, whereas an upthrust of the same size on the (immersed) beach-ball was large enough to push up the ball further out of the water. However, if the same plasticine lump is modelled into a boat which is able to displace as much water or more than the floating ball, it will float.

An object will sink when placed gently on calm water if it does not displace enough water for the upthrust of the water to balance the downward force of the object's weight. An object which is heavier than the weight of water it displaces will sink. Other objects can float.

Arm-bands for swimmers and life-jackets contain air (or another very light material), like the beach-ball above, so they float in a similar way. If pulled downward by the weight of a swimmer, in the same way as for the ball in Figure 9.7(c), more upthrust is produced. The extra upthrust on the arm-bands added to the upthrust on the swimmer's body is enough to balance his or her weight (the force downward) and to keep the swimmer afloat. As long as they are worn correctly, firmly above the elbows, they should keep the swimmer afloat. Water-rings do the same job, but unless they are kept in position under the armpits they can cause the bather to float upside-down in the water. With all swimming floats, large inflatable water toys, lilos and dinghies, if they are used in the sea the great danger is that the bather will be swept out to sea and drowned.

FORCES ALWAYS COME IN PAIRS

When you strike a tennis ball with a racquet, the ball changes speed and direction and the racquet is knocked backwards. When the racquet exerts a force on the ball, the ball exerts a force on the racquet. Forces always occur in pairs – weight and upthrust in the case of the floating beach-ball (page 137).

Suppose someone is holding one end of a strong spring, and you pull the free end. The spring will stretch because you are pulling it, but you will also feel a force pulling you towards the other person. You are exerting a force on the spring but the spring is also exerting a force in the opposite direction on you. The two forces balance. Likewise, the other person will be pulling back on the spring and will feel the pull of the spring on him: another pair of forces. Similarly, if you sit on a thick cushion your weight will push it down, but as the cushion is compressed it will push upwards on you until your weight (downwards) is the same as the cushion's force (upwards). In each case, the two forces are said to be balanced.

So whenever you exert a force on something, that something exerts the same size of force on you, but in the opposite direction.

FALLING OBJECTS – AIR RESISTANCE

The nearest we get to a single force acting alone on an object on Earth is when gravity pulls down and there is almost no force upwards to support it: the object is falling. Even so, air does push upwards; but the effects of air resistance can be reduced. Air resistance is most noticeable if the falling object is light and if it presents a large surface area to the air below it. A sheet of paper dropped as in Figure 9.10 illustrates this. In (a) the paper is rather like a parachute, designed to take advantage of the air slowing something down; (b) is like a diver trying to 'slice through' the surface on entry into the water to reduce drag from the water. However, a plastic plate is heavy enough for it not to be held back much by air resistance, whichever way it falls.

Figure 9.10

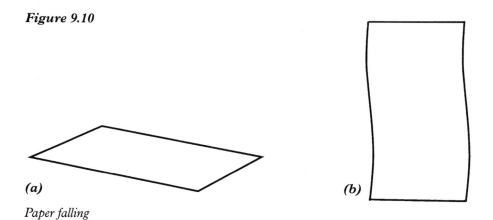

(a)   *(b)*

Paper falling

To minimise the effect of the air slowing down an object, choose something which is compact and preferably 'streamlined', to 'cut through' the air, and which is heavy, so that the upward force of the air resistance is small compared to the big weight downwards. A lump of plasticine with a streamlined shape does well. Even a paperclip, drawing pin or ballpoint pen is likely to reach the ground before an open paper tissue or a feather. (If an object falls far enough through the air it actually reaches a steady speed, beyond which it does not accelerate. This can be seen when a paper parachute is dropped from a height, but not with many other objects.) If the retarding effect of air friction (air resistance) has been almost eliminated, you can see the effect of almost a single force on an object. The object's weight (gravity) pulls it down and it falls faster and faster. A single force, or an unbalanced force, on an object causes it to accelerate.

Children might want to find out what happens if two objects of different weight are dropped at the same time. Does the heavier one reach the ground first? Unless air resistance has a great effect, the answer is 'No' – because two effects of the amount of 'stuff' an object is made of (its mass) work in opposite ways:

1 The larger the mass the bigger the force downwards (weight), so you might expect the larger mass to pick up speed faster. But . . .
2 the larger the mass of the object the more inertia it has, so the more difficult it is to make it pick up speed quickly, i.e. to accelerate quickly.

Effects 1 and 2 cancel one another. So two objects of different mass dropped at the same time fall together, picking up speed together. The larger mass is pulled harder by the Earth's gravity but its large mass makes it difficult to accelerate. The smaller mass is pulled gently by the Earth's gravity, but its small mass makes it relatively easy to accelerate.

So if any two compact, fairly heavy objects are dropped at the same time, they pick up speed, or accelerate, identically, reaching the ground at the same time.

FRICTION BETWEEN SOLIDS

Whenever you try to move one surface along another, a resisting force comes into play. This resisting force is called **friction**.

Just as a lawn always has small lumps and bumps, no matter how smooth it looks from a distance, so do apparently smooth surfaces. You can see these bumps on really rough surfaces like sandpaper. Even a mirror, a freshly polished car, a non-stick frying pan, may look 'perfectly' smooth; but with a powerful enough microscope we can see that those surfaces do have irregularities. Incidentally, two surfaces sliding over one another often knock tiny fragments off each surface, creating dust. We call this 'wear and tear'. This is how clothing wears out, as do many parts of a car or a sewing machine.

Consider dragging a table across a floor. If a small horizontal force is applied to the table, a frictional force comes into play which balances the applied force. The table does not move. As the applied force is gradually increased, the friction also increases. But there comes a stage when the force of friction reaches its maximum. If the applied force is increased even further, it will become large enough to 'overcome' friction and the table will slide over the floor. A frictional force is acting on the base of the table legs in the opposite direction to the movement of the table. So friction is a force which comes into play when one surface is made to slide over another (Figure 9.11). The force of friction acts in the opposite direction to the motion and can prevent movement altogether. If it is acting between moving surfaces, the frictional force can slow down the motion.

Figure 9.11

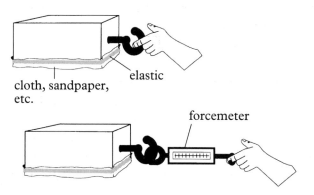

cloth, sandpaper,
etc.

Investigating the force of (solid) friction

If someone sits on the table, so that a larger force pushes down, the frictional force increases – you would have to exert a larger force to start it moving.

It is worth noting that friction plays a different role when an object rolls rather than slides. Rolling takes place only when there is a frictional force, e.g. between the roller, or wheels, and the ground; otherwise skidding occurs (see the diagram of the pushed bicycle in Figure 9.2(d)).

KEEPING GOING

Forcemeters can be used to find the forces necessary to pull toy vehicles and other objects along. An object needs a push or a pull to start it moving. Do moving things need a force to keep them going? Many people, of all ages, think they do, and that is not surprising. Most of the moving things we see slow down and stop unless they are pushed or pulled along. A bicycle will slow down and stop unless you keep pedalling. Roll a ball over the lawn and it will come to a halt. Can you think of anything which has no forces pushing or pulling it, but which does keep going once it has started to move? Not on Earth, perhaps. But what about out in space?

Spaceships, after being launched and getting far enough away, have their driving power turned off (sometimes by remote control) and cruise along at vast speeds without slowing down. Space probe Voyager II was launched from Earth using the forces of powerful engines. Then its direction was adjusted using smaller engines – sideways forces were used to alter the route it took. When it was far enough away, all the engine's forces acting on it were cut off – the engines were shut down. Did Voyager suddenly halt? No, it kept cruising at over 30,000 miles per hour until two years later it arrived near Jupiter, still travelling at the same speed!

So why can't a ball keep rolling on the lawn? Well, no matter how beautifully mown, the blades of grass that stick up get in the ball's way as would any little lumps and bumps. They'd each exert a force on the ball, slowing it down. Out in space, well away from planets, stars, meteors and so on, not only is there no grass but no lumps or bumps of any kind. No forces at all. Nothing to slow anything down. Now, many years after its launch, and with no forces acting on it, the space probe is still voyaging on at a steady speed. It would need a backward force to slow it down and stop it. On Earth, the best we can do to simulate a situation in which no forces are acting is to balance the force of gravity with an equal upward force, and to minimise frictional effects.

A hovercraft floats on a cushion of air with only a little friction between it and the air under it. It is fairly easy to make a balloon-hovercraft and great fun to experiment with it (Figure 9.12). All of the 'changes in movement' of the bicycle shown in Figure 9.3 are easy and fun to show. But the hovercraft is especially useful for showing the effect of having almost no friction.

Once the hovercraft is 'floating' over a smooth surface, a flick or a sharp tug horizontally will get it moving – and it will continue with an almost steady speed until it hits something or the balloon is deflated. When there are no forces acting on a moving object it will keep going at a steady speed indefinitely. A force is not needed to keep a friction-free object moving. In order to slow or stop a moving object, a force must be applied in the opposite direction to the movement.

What happens when you keep pulling on a friction-free moving object? Once friction has been removed, and a single force is applied continuously to an object, the object goes faster and faster – it accelerates. This is true of objects like the hovercraft which are pulled horizontally by a steady force. It is the case for falling objects (if compact and heavy enough) where the weight is the steady force. A steady force acting on a friction-free object which is free to move makes it move faster and faster. It accelerates.

Figure 9.12

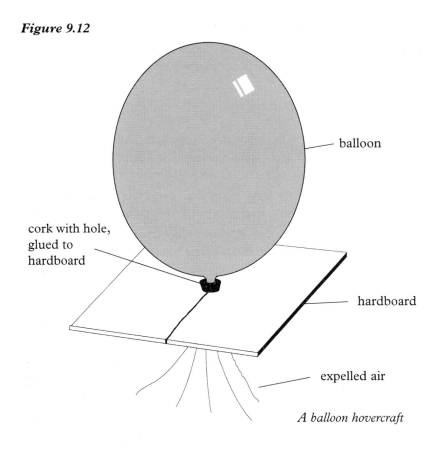

balloon

cork with hole,
glued to
hardboard

hardboard

expelled air

A balloon hovercraft

SPEED

Speed is a measure of how far something travels in a certain time. Very few objects maintain an entirely steady speed. So strictly speaking, any measurements we make will give average speeds. Speed is found by dividing the distance travelled by the time taken. The most familiar unit of speed is likely to be 'miles per hour', but for most measurements in the classroom, playground or sports field, times will be measured with stopwatches in seconds (converting from minutes as necessary).

Track events on sports day provide opportunities for calculating individuals' speeds in various events. However, since distances are pre-set, the times of individual performances will vary – many of those times being 'awkward' divisors, like 53 seconds. For easier division, get children (with bicycles or skateboards), toy cars, and so on, to move for a carefully chosen time which gives an easy divisor. Then measure the distance travelled, in metres, along the path taken by the moving object. Divide the distance travelled by the time taken, to get the average speed. To enable comparisons to be made, do all the calculations in the same units, e.g. metres and seconds.

SUMMARY

- A force is a push or a pull.
- Forces can be exerted directly by contact (e.g. when pushing a pram or towing a car) or through space (e.g. when a magnet attracts an iron nail).
- Forces can make an object twist, squash, stretch, break or tear. In other words, forces can change the shape of an object.
- A force is needed to make an object start to move, to make it go faster, slow it down, stop it or make it change direction. In other words, a force is needed to change the movement of an object. If something is not moving, we can in almost every case conclude that the forces acting in each direction on the stationary object balance one another. A stationary object which has no force at all acting on it will not move. Without a force to slow down a moving object (i.e. 'change its movement'), the object will carry on going straight at a steady speed. Applying a single force to it would make it go faster and faster – i.e. accelerate – or decelerate, or change direction, depending on the direction of that force.
- Forces always occur in pairs. If I exert a force on you, you will exert a force of the same size on me, although it will be in the opposite direction.
- If two compact, relatively heavy objects are dropped at the same time, they each pick up speed at the same rate, reaching the ground together – even if their weights differ.
- The Earth's gravity pulls all objects toward the centre of the Earth – holding objects on its surface and pulling down falling objects. We call the force of gravity on an object its weight.
- Magnetic forces also act through space. A north pole attracts a south pole, but two similar poles (both south poles or both north poles) repel each other. A magnet will attract iron and other magnetic materials.
- When forces are applied to two surfaces in contact, to make them slide over one another, the force of friction comes into play. It acts against the direction of movement, slowing objects down, and can prevent movement altogether. Friction can be a hindrance in some cases, but a help in others. Friction forces are needed for rolling to occur.

10

Light

JENNY KENNEDY

Introduction   150

Safety   150

Brightness   151

Darkness   151

Interpreting scientific diagrams of light   151

Light travels in straight lines   152

Transparency   152

Opaque materials and shadows   153

Reflection and how we see objects   154

Mirrors   156

How we see an image in a flat mirror   156

The speed of light   159

Summary   160

10

LIGHT

JENNY KENNEDY

INTRODUCTION

In this book light and sound have been treated separately, with comparisons made between them in the Summary. There are two main reasons for this: first, it was felt that most teachers at primary level would teach light and sound separately. For that approach, the layout facilitates quick and easy reference. Secondly, it is only at a more advanced stage that the wave-nature of both light and sound is encountered. Without that link there is no compelling reason for combining the two in one chapter.

Many of the practical exercises with light which accompany this text are best done in the dark. They are not designed as activities for pupils. However, if you wish to use them in the classroom, it may be helpful to screen off a dark corner for pupils' use.

It is convenient to show the direction in which light travels by drawing thin beams or rays. Although almost all light sources give out rays in many directions, diagrams would become very confused if many rays were drawn. Usually only one or two carefully selected rays are shown.

SAFETY

There are three major aspects of safety which must be observed when studying a variety of light sources such as candles, sparklers, torches, cycle lamps, household lights, street lights, car headlights, security lights, light-emitting diodes and so on. Children should be warned not to stare at bright lights, especially **not the Sun** – even using filters, ski goggles, sun specs, smoked glass, etc. Optical instruments like binoculars or telescopes can be especially dangerous. Secondly, many sources of light are hot, so pupils will need close supervision, especially where there are naked flames. Matches should be checked to ensure that pupils do not take them for fire-lighting elsewhere.

Thirdly, children should be supervised if using mains electricity, perhaps for a table lamp.

BRIGHTNESS

The brightness of a light source depends on how much light energy it sends out every second: that is, how powerful it is. We are familiar with the unit in which power is measured, the watt. It is used in rating household bulbs. Although we use that as an indication of how bright a bulb will glow (if used with our electricity mains), strictly speaking the wattage indicates how much electrical energy each second is needed to run the bulb – and much of that is wasted as heat and so does not contribute to the brightness of the light. Fluorescent tubes and halogen bulbs waste far less energy. A 15 watt fluorescent tube can be as bright as a 60 watt bulb – and the lower rating indicates it is more economical in its use of energy and so cheaper to run.

The brightness of a non-luminous surface depends on how much light energy each second is reflected from that surface. This will depend not only on the shininess and colour of the surface, but on its distance from a light source, the brightness of the source and the angle at which the light strikes the surface.

DARKNESS

We can only see an object if light from it reaches our eyes. If no light enters our eyes, either from a light source or from something which reflects light into our eyes, we see nothing at all: it is pitch black. In general, we can say that darkness is 'no light' or the absence of light. (See 'Reflection and how we see objects', pages 154–5).

INTERPRETING SCIENTIFIC DIAGRAMS OF LIGHT

When diagrams are used to help explain how light behaves, it is often assumed that there is only one source of light – perhaps a torch. This means that if you want to set up equipment to see for yourself the effects shown in a diagram, you might need to cut out all other light and work in a darkened (or very dim) area.

You will be familiar with the idea of beams of light. Most beams from torches, lighthouses, and so on, spread out in straight lines from their source, like water from a shower-head. However, sometimes light travels in a parallel beam, like a searchlight. In diagrams we use straight lines to represent 'rays' of light, which are very fine parallel-sided beams. An arrow indicates the direction in which the light is travelling out from the source. When a diagram is used to illustrate a particular idea – perhaps to do with shadow formation, or reflection from a mirror – only a few, carefully selected rays are drawn. (There will be innumerable other ones which could be added, but this would cause confusion.)

LIGHT TRAVELS IN STRAIGHT LINES

The section in this chapter on 'Opaque materials and shadows' (pages 153–4) gives hints on how to produce sharply defined shadows. If light did not travel in straight lines, it would wander sideways into the shadow and the shadow would be blurred. You would be unable to produce sharp shadows at all.

TRANSPARENCY

When hitting an object, light can be absorbed by the material, transmitted through it, or reflected by it. Perhaps the most obviously transparent materials are colourless glass and some plastics, water and air. Flat, clean panes of glass or plastic let the light through so well that they often go unnoticed – people regularly walk into glass doors, and they slip and skid on unseen patches of water. Coloured transparent materials (e.g. toffee papers) can be used to filter (allow through) different colours of light.

Most ordinary bulbs send out all of the colours of the rainbow, which we perceive as yellow or white light. A red filter absorbs all the colours in white light except red, which passes through, so that we see a red bulb.

Translucent materials, like greaseproof paper, baking parchment and the glass of pearl light bulbs, let some but not all light through – they scatter or diffuse the light.

OPAQUE MATERIALS AND SHADOWS

Most of the objects around us are made of materials which are entirely opaque to light. Any light falling on an opaque object is blocked by it, with some of the light bouncing back, and some is absorbed. If there are no other light sources, a shadow may be formed.

The word 'shadow' is commonly used in two slightly different ways. It is used when light falls on to an object to describe that part of the object itself which receives no light. We talk of the unlit surface of the Moon, for example, as being 'in shadow'. However, we often talk of shadows as being cast on to the ground or a wall. In the case of the Moon, its shadow is cast out into space and for most of the time isn't 'cast' on to another object. Consider first the shadow of a doll cast by a small or masked bulb, on to a wall in an otherwise dark room (Figure 10.1(a)). Light will shine out from the bulb in all directions. All the rays hitting the doll are stopped from travelling on to the wall. No light falls on the part of the wall directly behind the doll, and a sharp shadow forms.

A screen of translucent material, such as baking parchment, allows some light to pass through it. Shadows cast on to it can be seen from both sides – this is useful if the audience is large, or if the shadow but not the doll is to be seen, so pupils can guess what the object is.

In order to vary the size of the shadow, change the distance between light source and doll, or doll and wall (Figure 10.1(b) and (c)). Of course, a brighter bulb gives a deeper shadow.

Figure 10.1(d), which uses a large torch and no mask, shows what happens if you use an extended light source. The rays from the centre of the filament are equivalent to those from a small bulb. Additionally, there are rays bouncing off the reflector around the bulb. These partly illuminate the former dark area, causing the outline of the shadow to become blurred. This happens all around the shadow. For sharp shadows keep the light source small compared to the object – or move the larger bulb further away, though this has the disadvantage of lessening the contrast between light and dark areas of the screen.

Figure 10.1

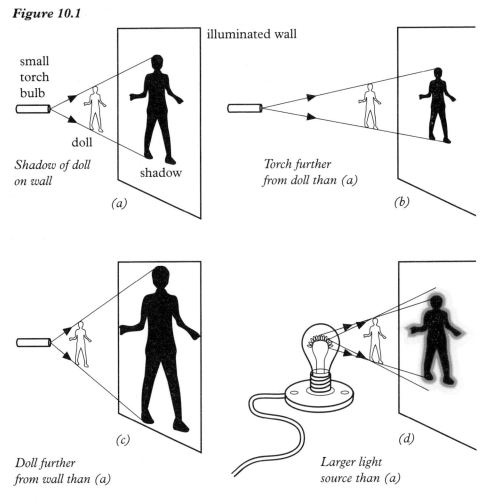

small
torch
bulb

doll

illuminated wall

*Shadow of doll
on wall*

shadow

(a)

*Torch further
from doll than (a)*

(b)

*Doll further
from wall than (a)*

(c)

*Larger light
source than (a)*

(d)

Shadows

REFLECTION AND HOW WE SEE OBJECTS

It is important for pupils to realise that they can see an object only if light
from the object enters their eyes. Many children believe that light emanates
from their eyes, causing objects to be visible. Pupils could be asked to give
lists of things which give out their own light so that we can see them, even
when it is otherwise dark. Their suggestions for sources of light are likely to
include the TV, household lights, torches, the Sun and electric eels, and
some of their drawings of these light sources will probably show rudimentary
'rays' of light.

However, most of the things around us that we see are not self-luminous: they do not have their own light. When light falls on to a non-luminous object, several things can happen. If the object is transparent (e.g. a window), light passes through it. If the object is opaque (like our bodies) some of the light falling on it will be absorbed by the object. Also, some of the light hitting any object will bounce off it, and then we say that that light has been reflected.

We can see non-luminous objects only if light from a light source bounces from them into our eyes (Figure 10.2). The object that we see is reflecting the light. Most objects are not smooth and glossy like mirrors, but have textured surfaces of varying roughness. Because of this, light is reflected from their surfaces in all directions: we say that the light is scattered. It is by scattered light that we are able to see most objects around us: other people, houses, books, cats, everything except light sources.

Figure 10.2

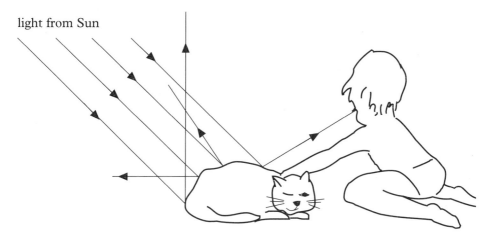

light from Sun

Light scatters from a cat so it can be seen from all directions

'Reflections' are probably associated, in many people's minds, with reflections in calm water. This is a special case of reflection, where there is a mirror-like surface, and upside-down images of trees, boats and ducks are seen. However, it is important to realise that light bounces off (is reflected by) almost all surfaces, not just mirrors. ('Almost' all is necessary, because matt or dull black surfaces absorb all the light that falls on them.)

MIRRORS

A mirror has a particularly smooth and shiny reflecting surface. Because of that, light is not scattered off it in all directions. On the contrary, it is easy to predict exactly the one direction in which a particular ray of light will be reflected from a mirror. Figure 10.3(a) shows a vertical flat mirror, the back of which is indicated by shading. A ray of light is bouncing off its front surface. The angle which the reflected ray makes with the mirror is the same size as the angle at which the ray hits the mirror, no matter how big that angle is. Also, since the ray hitting the mirror is travelling horizontally along the page, the reflected ray is also in the plane of the page. It doesn't 'poke out' of the page. (For more advanced work the angle the ray makes with the perpendicular to the mirror is used.)

Figure 10.3

back of mirror

The angles made by a ray of light before and after hitting a flat mirror are the same size

It may not be obvious to children that we can only see ourselves in a mirror if we are illuminated. When we 'look in a mirror' light is being reflected – first from us and then from the mirror.

HOW WE SEE AN IMAGE IN A FLAT MIRROR

Light travels in straight lines. Rays coming from behind us don't bend around our heads and enter our eyes, so we can't see things which are behind us. Our eyes receive rays from objects in front of us. The rays have travelled straight from the object into our eyes. We are so used to this that if light happens to be bent before reaching our eyes, we are fooled. We 'think' the position of the object which sends light into our eyes can be traced back along the light rays in straight lines. This is how we see an 'image' in a different place from the object.

When we see ourselves in a flat mirror we rely on light, perhaps from a light bulb, to illuminate our face. In Figure 10.4 those rays are not shown. Our face then scatters that light on to the mirror. The mirror reflects light back. Only three rays of light from a spot on the face are shown being reflected by the mirror. These include one ray which enters the person's eye. We can ignore the other two rays.

Figure 10.4

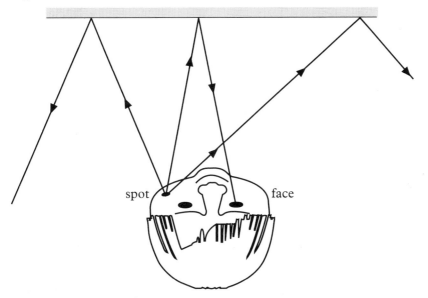

Some rays of light scattered from a spot on the face being reflected from a flat mirror

Figure 10.5 shows how two rays from the spot, entering the eyes after reflection from the mirror, locate the image of the spot. Actually, of course, many rays would bounce from the mirror into each eye but it would be difficult to draw them very close together without muddling the diagram. Our brains are used to our eyes receiving rays which have travelled straight from an object into our eyes. When a ray enters our eye, we assume it has travelled in a straight line – even if in fact it has bounced off a mirror and changed direction.

Figure 10.5 shows someone using a mirror to examine a spot. Lots of rays scattered from the spot will hit the mirror, but only two have been drawn; one

Figure 10.5

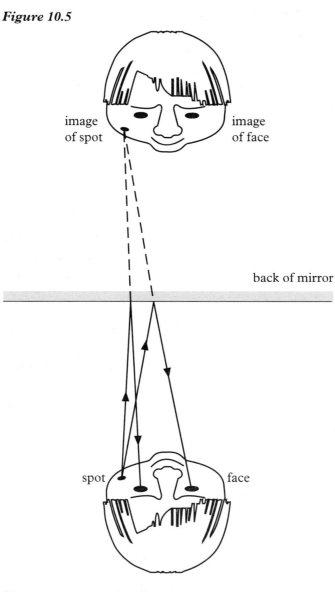

How we see an image in a flat mirror

of which enters each eye after being reflected off the mirror. The brain assumes that those rays have come straight, so they seem to have come along the dotted paths. The spot seems to be behind the mirror, at the point where the dotted lines meet.

Similarly, a pair of rays could be drawn from all other points on the face, showing how the whole image of the face is formed. Notice that the image of the face is the same size as the original, and it is as far behind the mirror as the actual face is in front of it.

Curved mirrors are great fun, giving enlarged or reduced images, sometimes upside-down, and usually distorted. Look into shiny spoons, tins and smooth kitchen foil – get really close and then far away, to note the differences in the images you see.

THE SPEED OF LIGHT

Nothing in the whole universe travels faster than light when it is passing through completely empty space, although other forms of radiation do travel at the same speed. (The other radiations are known as gamma-radiation, X-radiation, ultra-violet radiation, infra-red radiation, microwave-radiation and radio-radiation. Note that sound is not included in this list.) Sound cannot travel through empty space – it depends on molecules in materials to pass vibrations on. As can be seen in Table 10.1, light travels much, much faster than sound. (The speed of each in fact depends on the material through which it passes.) Light travels nearly a million times further in a second than sound does.

Because of this, in a thunderstorm, when thunder and lightning are produced simultaneously, the light from the lightning reaches us before the sound of the thunder. When, at the far end of a large field, a cricket bat strikes a ball, we see the strike before we hear it.

Table 10.1 Speeds in metres per second

Light (in air)	300 million
Sound (in air)	330
Land speed record	331
Fastest bird (peregrine falcon swooping)	47
Britain's motorway speed limit	33
Fastest land animal (cheetah)	27
Fastest sprint (human)	12

It is fun for able pupils to work out how long it takes light from the Sun to reach us, 93 million miles or 150 million kilometres away. It is about eight minutes, even at its tremendously fast speed. That means that we see the Sun as it was eight minutes ago, not as it is now. The Sun is our nearest star, and from the next nearest star light takes four years to reach us. The most distant object in the universe detected by modern instruments is so far away that its light takes thousands of millions of years to reach us. We see it as it was thousands of millions of years ago, and would have to wait for thousands of millions more years to find out what it looks like 'now'.

SUMMARY

- Light and sound are both forms of energy. The more intense the source the more energy is emitted – the brighter the light or the louder the sound.
- Light and sound travel in straight lines. Because of this our eyes and ears can locate the source of light or sound. Both light and sound can pass through some substances (e.g. air, water) but many objects which allow sound to pass through them are opaque to light (e.g. walls, string).
- Light and sound can both be reflected, producing, respectively, images in mirrors and echoes from hard surfaces.
- Light travels nearly a million times faster than sound. Nothing travels faster than light.

11

Sound

GEOFFREY WICKHAM

Making a sound   162

The transmission of sound   164

Sound waves   166

Frequency and pitch   168

Loudness and amplitude   169

Timbre   170

Noise control   170

Summary   171

11

SOUND

GEOFFREY WICKHAM

MAKING A SOUND

There may seem to be little in common between a toddler screaming in a supermarket and the Berlin Philharmonic Orchestra playing Beethoven, but the way in which the sound is made, transmitted and detected is common to both. The message may be different but the medium is the same. All sound, whether noise or music, is produced by something vibrating. This causes the air in contact with the object to vibrate, and this vibration is transmitted through the air until, on reaching the ear, it sets the ear-drum vibrating. These vibrations are converted into electrical impulses and interpreted by the brain. We are bombarded by a multitude of sounds, noises, sweet harmonies and grating discords in everyday life, but they can all be sorted into a few basic means of production.

Ways of making a sound

Striking A baby soon discovers that one of the simplest ways of making sound is by striking one object against another. Homes are full of such sounds, from baby dropping a hard toy out of the cot again, to the slam of doors and the clatter of pots and pans in the kitchen. As a result of the latter, the percussion section of the orchestra has been called the 'kitchen' section. It includes drums of many types, cymbals, tambourines, triangles and other instruments, most of which produce a noise rather than a note of definite pitch. In addition there are the percussion instruments which give definite notes: xylophones, bells, chime bars and kettledrums (timpani). Similar instruments are found in many cultures, ranging from gamelan orchestras in Bali, with their many tuned gongs and bells, to steel-drum bands in the West Indies and the marimbas of Africa.

It is easy to show that these all vibrate when making a sound. When sounding loudly the surface of many of them looks blurred, and when sounding quietly small pieces of paper dropped on their surfaces will jump, showing that they are vibrating.

Wires or strings A stretched string or wire produces a musical note when hit (piano) or plucked (guitar, harp, harpsichord). Once the note sounds it immediately begins to fade away, but a continuous sound can be made by stroking the string with a rosined bow, as with instruments of the violin family. If you drop small V-shaped pieces of paper on the strings while they are sounding they jump off, showing that they are vibrating.

Air columns Blowing across the top of a bottle causes the air in the bottle to vibrate, producing a musical note: the larger the bottle the deeper the note. Instruments that depend on a column of air being vibrated in this way include the tin whistle, recorder, flute and pipe organ, in which some pipes are open at the end (like a recorder), giving a bright sound, and others are closed (like pan pipes), giving a mellow sound (Figure 11.1).

Figure 11.1

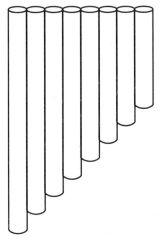

Pan pipes

There are two further ways in which a column of air can be vibrated. Most children have held a piece of grass tautly between the thumbs and blown through them to produce a sound. The vibrations of the grass are clearly felt as a tingling in the thumbs (Figure 11.2). If you imagine making this noise over the top of a tube, you have the basis of reed instruments such as clarinets, oboes and saxophones. More importantly, it is how the human voice is produced. The larynx contains the vocal cords: two thin pieces of tissue which are brought into close contact when the voice is used and which vibrate when air is forced through them from the lungs. You can feel the vibrations by holding the throat and humming or singing.

Figure 11.2

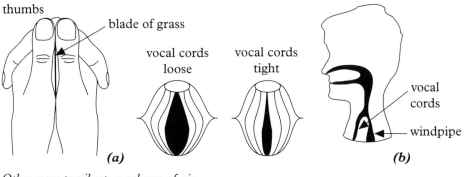

Other ways to vibrate a column of air
(a) Blowing grass between the thumbs
(b) Vocal cords

The final way to vibrate a column of air is by putting the lips close together and blowing to produce the elegant version of the 'raspberry' which activates brass instruments from bugle to tuba.

Loudspeakers In this list of sound producers, the one most likely to be over-looked has become the most commonplace: the vibrating cone of cardboard which is the sound producer (or reproducer) in the loudspeaker. If you take a loudspeaker out of its case and support it with the vibrating surface horizontal, a table tennis ball on the vibrating surface will dance to a tune.

THE TRANSMISSION OF SOUND

Although we have thought so far of sound travelling through air, sound can also travel through solids. Few teachers need reminding that sound can travel through classroom walls and closed windows. Stories abound of prisoners communicating with those in other cells by tapping on water pipes or on the wall.

A toy, familiar to many children, which demonstrates sound travelling along a solid is the string telephone. This consists of two flexible discs (tin lids or yoghurt pots) joined by a long piece of string pulled tight (Figure 11.3). A child talking into one end can be heard by a child using the other disc as an earpiece. The string needs to be long enough for the two to be out of immediate earshot of each other.

Sound can also travel through liquids, a fact of less importance to humans

Figure 11.3

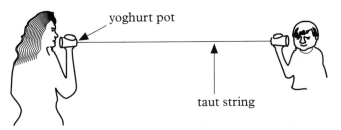

yoghurt pot

taut string

A string telephone

than to dolphins, which communicate with each other through water by a high-pitched chattering sound. The transmission of sound through water has become an important part of navigation. The depth of water can be found by echo-sounding (Figure 11.4). A high-pitched note is sent out by a transmitter in the hull of the ship, and the echo from the sea bed is picked up by a receiver. The depth of water can be worked out from the time it takes for the echo to return. Similar devices have also been used to pick up the sound of enemy submarines.

Figure 11.4

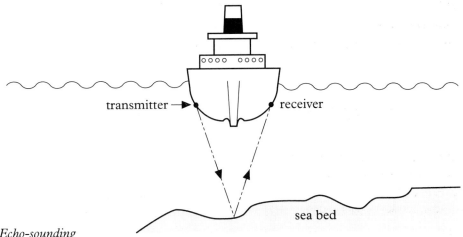

transmitter → receiver

sea bed

Echo-sounding

Since sound travels by vibration, where there is nothing to vibrate there can be no sound: in other words, sound cannot travel through completely empty space – what we call a vacuum. Sound differs in this respect from light: we can see the light and feel the heat from the Sun, but the immense noise which the Sun must produce cannot travel through the empty space to Earth.

Figure 11.5

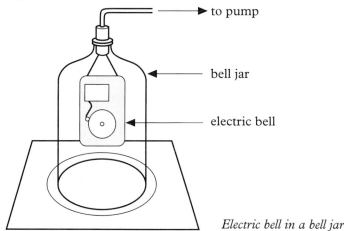

to pump

bell jar

electric bell

Electric bell in a bell jar

This was demonstrated over three hundred years ago by pumping the air from a glass bottle in which a clockwork bell was suspended (Figure 11.5). The sound steadily decreased and almost disappeared. There was still a faint sound because the pump could not produce a perfect vacuum.

There is so little atmosphere on the Moon that astronauts standing close to each other on its surface would be unable to hear each other, no matter how hard they shouted. There is very little gas between their helmets to carry the sound. They have to use radio links to talk to each other. If their radios failed, their only way of talking would be by touching helmets and using the transmission of sound through the solid material of these.

SOUND WAVES

In solids, liquids and gases, sound travels by means of sound waves, but these are of a different kind to water waves which move up and down as the wave passes by. If they are gentle waves and not breakers, a cork placed on the water will just bob up and down in the same place. Sound waves work in a different way.

When a drum skin vibrates outwards it compresses the air next to it. If we imagine the air being in layers, the layers nearest to the drum skin are pushed close together. These layers will, in turn, press the air further out, and the sudden compression of the air will travel through it like a shock wave (Figure 11.6). This continues while the drum is vibrating. The air itself does not move

Figure 11.6

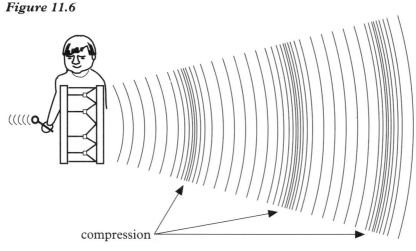

compression

Sound waves

along in one direction: it only vibrates backwards and forwards in the same place.

The effect can be seen easily if you have a long spring. Toy shops sell them for the fun of getting them to 'walk' downstairs. If it is stretched and held at each end, and one person gives it a quick jerk backwards and forwards, a wave can be seen to travel down the length of the spring (Figure 11.7). If you stick a paper clip on the spring you will see that it vibrates back and forth. So each bit of the spring just vibrates back and forth but is playing a part in passing the wave down the spring. In this it resembles a human chain passing buckets of water from a pond to put out a fire. Each human vibrates to and fro, but the buckets flow in one direction. Air vibrates back and forth just like that when a sound passes through it.

Figure 11.7

this hand shakes
back and forth   a wave moves along the spring   this hand is still

Waves in a spring

When a stone is thrown into the middle of a pond, the ripples become fainter the further out they travel. In a similar way, sound waves become fainter the further they travel from the source.

How fast are sound waves?

We are so used to sound and sight synchronising, except when a film projector is faulty, that it still comes as a slight surprise to see a distant figure hit a post with a mallet and hear the sound later. Such experiences make it obvious that it takes an appreciable time for sound to travel. Echoes are also an illustration of this. Just as light can be reflected by a mirror, so sound can be reflected by a hard surface. An echo will be heard a whole second later if it rebounds from a wall or rock face about 165 m away. In other words, the sound has travelled to and from the rock, a total of 330 m in a second. So the speed of sound in air is about 330 m per second.

By comparison, the speed of light is much greater, about 300 million m per second; so for most practical purposes on Earth, the time taken for light to travel can be ignored. Radio waves travel at the same speed as light, so someone listening to the radio in Australia will hear the chimes of Big Ben marginally before a tourist gazing up at it from Parliament Square. The radio waves will take about a tenth of a second to reach Australia; the sound waves, travelling much more slowly, will take about half a second to reach Parliament Square.

People are most aware of how much slower sound travels than light in a thunderstorm. Some nervously count the time between the flash of lightning and the clap of thunder as a rough guide to the distance away of the storm: 1 kilometre for every 3 seconds or 1 mile for every 5 seconds.

FREQUENCY AND PITCH

When you switch on a vacuum cleaner the motor takes a second or two to reach full speed, and in that time its sound rises from a low hum to a high-pitched whine. The faster the motor vibrates, the higher the pitch of the sound. The same can be heard with any vibrating object, such as a car engine.

The number of vibrations per second is called the frequency. A child's ear can detect sounds from as low as 20 vibrations per second, which is a deep rumble, up to about 20,000, a very high-pitched whistle. The note in the middle of a piano keyboard, middle C, has a frequency of 256 vibrations per second. Dogs and cats can hear much higher frequencies than the human ear. Dog whistles make a sound which is called ultrasonic because, although dogs can hear it, humans cannot.

About 2,500 years ago the Greek mathematician Pythagoras made the discovery that there is an interesting connection between music and mathematics. If you play a note on a violin or guitar, and then play the note you get by stopping the string exactly halfway up, the new note is an octave higher. The string, at half its original length, is vibrating twice as fast. So, if middle C on the piano vibrates at 256 vibrations per second and you go up seven white piano keys to the next C, that will vibrate at 512 vibrations per second.

The note also depends on how tightly the string is stretched, that is, its tension: the higher the tension, the higher the note. It also depends on the thickness of the string: the thicker the string, the lower the note. Look inside a piano, or compare the top string on a violin with the lowest, and then compare that with the strings on a cello or double bass.

In a wind instrument the pitch depends on the length of tube, but it also depends on the pressure with which it is blown. A bugler can obtain several different notes from the bugle by altering the pressure of the lips on each other, although the length of tube does not alter. In a similar way woodwind instruments can give a series of different notes by overblowing.

LOUDNESS AND AMPLITUDE

One way of making a noise, as many children discover, is by holding one end of a ruler firmly on a table and twanging the other end. The loudness of the noise depends on how far down they pull the ruler before letting go.

In the same way, if you pluck a guitar string it will vibrate rapidly, and just look like a blur. The louder the note, the wider that blur will be (Figure 11.8). The height of the blur from the middle position is called the amplitude.

Figure 11.8

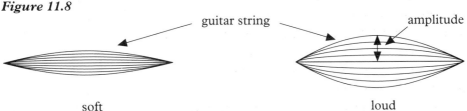

guitar string — amplitude

soft   loud

Waves at high and low amplitudes

Loudness, therefore, depends on the amplitude of the vibration. This applies to all forms of sound, even where, as with wind instruments, you cannot see the vibrations.

TIMBRE

When you hear a saxophone, recorder or guitar play a note, it is not a single pure note but a mixture of different notes: a bottom note (called the fundamental) and several higher notes (called overtones). It is this mixture that gives each instrument its own peculiar character, or timbre, so that a trumpet playing a note sounds different from a violin playing the same note.

NOISE CONTROL

Only in battle were previous generations bombarded with sound in the way we are now. For too many people the noise of heavy lorries, aeroplanes, machinery, children shouting and over-loud music is an unavoidable and often painful part of daily life.

Up to a certain level the ill-effects of noise are irritating rather than dangerous. It is less easy to work, sleep or just enjoy life in the midst of noise. The type of noise can be as important as its volume: the noise of a wasp in a bedroom may be more worrying than that of heavy lorries outside.

Beyond a certain level, noise is more than irritating: it can be painful and damaging. A few hours in a noisy factory or a disco may leave you with ringing and hissing noises in the ear. After a short time this will go, but if the exposure is repeated many times or the level of noise is exceptionally high, the damage will become worse and lasting.

There are two main ways to reduce the ill-effects of noise. One is to reduce the noise at source. This can be done by a number of means, including:

- designing quieter engines;
- banning night flights from airports between certain hours;
- controlling by law the level of noise that is allowed.

For example, certain public halls in residential areas are fitted with controls so that, if the band plays too loudly, the loudspeaker system automatically turns itself off.

The other way is by reducing the level of sound that reaches the ear. This may mean:

- ear protection for workers in heavy industry and musicians in rock bands;
- double glazing of houses and offices near heavy traffic;
- putting up noise barriers such as fences, or planting trees and shrubs for people living near motorways.

The level of noise is measured in decibels. The human ear begins to register sound at 0 decibels, and at about 120 to 130 decibels noise becomes painful. Table 11.1 gives the noise levels of several common sources. These figures are only a rough guide, because they will depend on how far away you are from the source of the sound.

Table 11.1 Noise level (in decibels) of everyday noises

Jet aircraft 40 m away	130
Thunder overhead	110
Jet aircraft overhead	100
Rock group	90
Traffic on a busy road	70
Conversation	60
Whisper	20

SUMMARY

- Sound can be produced in many ways, but they all involve something vibrating; such as a drum skin or a column of air as in a recorder.
- We normally think of sound travelling through air, but it can also travel through solids and liquids. Unlike light, it cannot travel through a vacuum.
- Sound travels in the form of sound waves. These are like shock waves in which the air vibrates back and forth, passing the sound on.
- These sound waves travel far more slowly than light, at about 330 metres per second.
- Whether the sound is high- or low-pitched depends on the frequency of the vibration: 20 vibrations per second will be a low rumble; 20,000 will be a very high-pitched whistle.
- The loudness will depend on the width of the vibration of the sound wave. Damage to hearing caused by excessive loudness is one of the hazards of modern life.

12

The Earth and Beyond

JIM JARDINE AND JENNY KENNEDY

Introduction   174

Sun, Earth and Moon   175

Finding south   179

The apparent path of the Sun (1)   180

Shadows cast by the Sun   181

Earth's tilt   184

The apparent path of the Sun (2)   186

Phases of the Moon   188

Summary   192

12

The Earth and Beyond

Jim Jardine
Jenny Kennedy

Introduction

Do not encourage anyone to look directly at the Sun, as this may damage their sight permanently. Many sunglasses offer no protection, and other filters, such as smoked glass and tissue paper, are not recommended. Optical instruments like telescopes and binoculars are particularly dangerous if used to look at the Sun.

This book has been written specifically to support the Science National Curriculum for Britain, so all references to observations from Earth (e.g. of the apparent path of the Sun across the sky) assume the observer to be in Britain.

Understanding the relative movements of the Sun, the Earth and its Moon presents several problems. One is that we are dealing with three-dimensional objects and so diagrams on a flat, two-dimensional page are often painfully inadequate. For a more realistic representation, you are advised to use a torch or slide projector to represent the Sun, and one sphere (perhaps a blue tennis ball) to represent the Earth and a smaller one (e.g. a white table-tennis ball) for the Moon. Use them in a darkened room or in a dull corner whenever you find a diagram difficult to interpret. It is as well to keep to a particular colour for any balls used to represent each of the heavenly bodies studied: yellow for Sun, blue for Earth, white for Moon.

Another difficulty is the variety of viewpoints we have to take, in order to explain observations made from Earth. Fortunately we get used at an early age to the idea of viewing the Earth from 'out in space', having become familiar with photographs of Earth taken from space, and with a globe of Earth on a stand.

Yet another problem is to do with the scale of diagrams. It is almost impossible to draw any diagram representing more than one 'heavenly body' using the same scale for both the size of the bodies and the distance between them. Table 12.1 gives some data for the Sun, Earth and Moon. From that you can work out that even if the Moon is represented on a scale diagram as a tiny circle of diameter only 3 mm, the Earth would be drawn with a diameter of 13 mm. They should then be drawn 0.4 m apart, but would not fit on to a sheet of A4 paper. There has therefore been no attempt at scale-drawing for the diagrams in this chapter.

Table 12.1 Data on Earth, Moon and Sun

	Diameter (thousand km)	Distance from Earth (million km)
Earth	13	—
Moon	3	0.4
Sun	1 400	150

The reason why capital letters are used for the Sun, Earth and Moon is that they are the proper names, specific to three particular bodies. There are other suns – many millions of them. Each star is a sun. The word 'planet' is used to describe a large body orbiting a star. The Earth is one of several planets orbiting our star, the Sun. A moon is a relatively small object orbiting a planet.

You will notice that in some of the following diagrams, rays from the Sun are shown parallel. Since the Sun is a round 'fireball', rays of light are actually travelling out in all directions – spreading out, or diverging, not parallel. So why are they often shown in the diagrams as parallel? If the Earth were very near the Sun then the rays which just skirt the Earth would be spreading out (see Figure 12.1). However, since the Earth is very distant from the Sun, the rays which just pass on either side of the Earth are much less divergent. If the Earth's distance from the Sun could be shown to the correct scale, those rays would be even more nearly parallel.

SUN, EARTH AND MOON

There are only two obvious natural objects in the sky which can look clearly circular to the naked eye: the Sun (seen through cloud or haze, but do not look!), and the Moon (when in the phase known as Full Moon). Artificial satellites are seen as discs too, but are much smaller than either the Sun or the Moon. Moving, coloured lights in the sky are likely to be the lights of aircraft.

The only solid shape for which the outline is circular, when viewed from

Figure 12.1

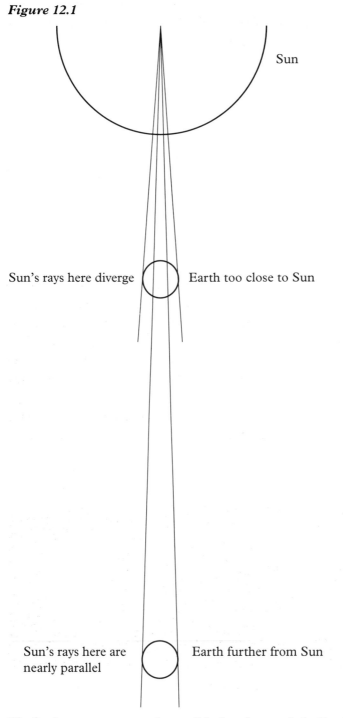

Sun

Sun's rays here diverge   Earth too close to Sun

Sun's rays here are   Earth further from Sun
nearly parallel

The Sun's rays are very nearly parallel when they reach the Earth

any direction, is the sphere. If we had no other evidence except that of direct observations from Earth, it is possible that the Sun or Moon could have one of a number of shapes (see Figure 12.2).

Figure 12.2

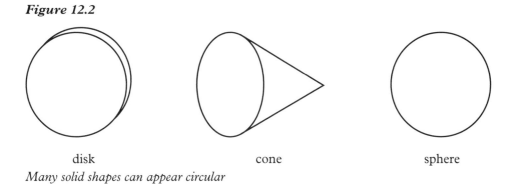

disk   cone   sphere

Many solid shapes can appear circular

It is just a fluke that the Sun and the Moon seem to us to be about the same size. The Sun's diameter is actually about 400 times the diameter of the Moon, but the Sun is roughly 400 times farther away from Earth than the Moon is (see Table 12.1). The Moon can therefore just cover the Sun. When it does so, it causes the total eclipse of the Sun, and only the outer flares of the Sun are seen. It happens when the Moon lines up exactly between the Sun and the Earth (see Figure 12.3).

The Sun, the Moon and the Earth all lie in approximately the same plane (see Figure 12.4). So the Sun and the Moon appear to us to take similar

Figure 12.3

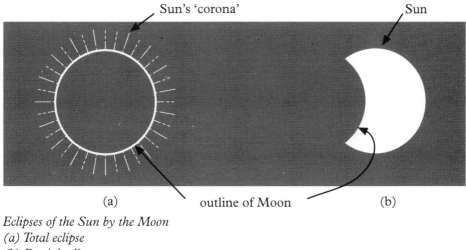

Sun's 'corona'   Sun

(a)   outline of Moon   (b)

Eclipses of the Sun by the Moon
(a) Total eclipse
(b) Partial eclipse

Figure 12.4

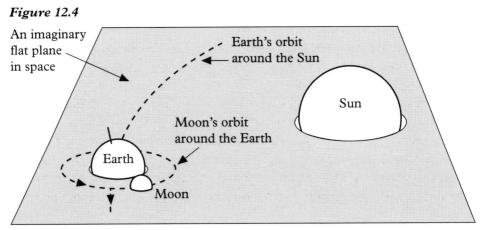

Sun, Moon and Earth all lie in approximately in the same plane

paths across the sky, moving in the same direction but at different rates. This means you know where to look for the Moon, either by day or by night. It is, for example, no good looking directly overhead, nor directly north. Also, when the Moon gets to the point closest to the Sun it will be obscured by the Sun's glare.

Sun

The Sun is a star, and like all stars we believe it to be an extremely hot sphere, consisting of individual atoms and parts of atoms. It is powered by nuclear reactions and emits its own light. The Sun's temperature at its core is probably greater than 14,000,000°C, and at its surface about 6,000°C.

Earth

The Earth has its own atmosphere, a layer of gases all around it. The Earth has been photographed from many angles, by space probes and by Earth satellites. Earth is roughly spherical, bulging slightly at the equator. However, some pupils are likely to cling to the idea of a flat or saucer-shaped Earth. Although composed mainly of solids, part of Earth's interior is hot, molten rock. About 70% of its surface area is covered by water. The Earth spins on its own axis, taking approximately 24 hours to do so. As different regions of the Earth turn to face the Sun, so they experience daytime.

Moon

Fortunately, the Moon has been seen and photographed from a number of different angles, by Moon probes. None of those photographs has led us to believe that the Moon is anything other than a large, dry, rocky sphere with no atmosphere. The Moon appears to us to travel in an arc across the sky, taking slightly less than 24 hours to complete one orbit of the Earth. The Moon always turns the same face to Earth so that we never see the far side of the Moon from Earth. It may be necessary to remind pupils that the Moon can sometimes be seen by day and sometimes by night. It emits no light of its own, and we see the Moon only by sunlight reflected from its surface.

FINDING SOUTH

In most of Britain for most of the day, you see the Sun in the southern part of the sky. How do we find out which direction is south? You can of course use a magnetic compass whose arrow-head will point north. Another way is to use the simplest of sundials. A stick pushed vertically into the ground will, around midday (adjusting for British Summer Time), cast its shadow more or less toward north. Looking in the opposite direction, toward but not directly at the Sun, you face the southern part of the sky. Draw a line on the ground along the shadow, with an arrow to show it points north (like arrows found on maps). Facing north you can't see the Sun without turning your head, except sometimes in early morning or late evening in summer. Turn around, to face the southern part of the sky, to see the Sun.

Rising above the horizon in the eastern part of the sky, the Sun seems to climb in a curve higher and higher, and to cast shorter and shorter shadows throughout the morning until, at midday, it is at its highest point, in the south (see Figure 12.5). It continues on its curved path casting longer and longer shadows, until it sinks in the west. Most children are aware that during the darkness of night the Sun is not visible, but some think it is hidden by a cloud or hill, rather than that it is still shining on the other side of the Earth.

THE APPARENT PATH OF THE SUN (1)

You will already be aware that, for an observer in Britain, the Sun seems to trace an arc in the southern part of the sky, from its eastern to its western part. The Sun's apparent path across the sky as seen from London at different parts of the year is shown in Figure 12.5.

Figure 12.5

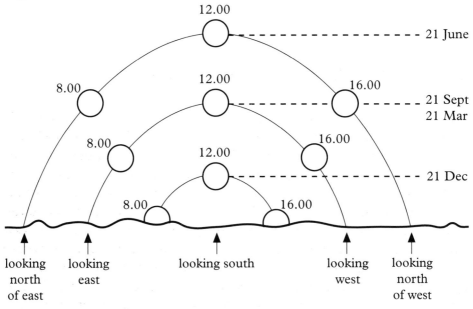

Changes in the Sun's apparent path throughout the year

Note the similarities in the paths of the Sun throughout the year:

- the Sun always rises in the eastern part of the sky;
- it climbs upwards on a curve in the southern part of the sky;
- it is highest in the sky at midday (allowing for British Summer Time);
- after noon, it traces a similar curve down towards the horizon in the western part of the sky.

Now note the differences in the paths of the Sun throughout the year:

- the Sun rises due east on only two days in the year: 21 March and 21 September, which are also the only days on which the Sun sets due west;
- during summer the Sun rises and sets in the northern half of our sky;

- the times for sunrise and sunset vary considerably throughout the year, so that the number of hours of sunlight in summer is much greater than in winter;
- at any particular time of day, the Sun is much higher in the sky in summer than in winter;
- between any two times of the day, the Sun seems to us to travel through a longer arc in the sky in summer than in winter. The Sun seems to travel faster and so change its position more quickly in summer than in winter.

SHADOWS CAST BY THE SUN

Do not encourage anyone to look directly at the Sun, as this could damage their sight permanently. Instead, study shadows formed by the Sun. A shadow is not an image. A shadow is formed when light falls onto an opaque object which prevents light reaching a surface, but light does pass by the object on to that surface. In both parts of Figure 12.6, the shadow of a tree is cast on to the ground. Sunlight falling on the tree is obstructed by the tree, whereas light passing over the tree illuminates the ground. By comparing the two parts of Figure 12.6 you see that when the Sun is high in the sky, the shadow is shorter than when the Sun is low. As the Sun moves around from east to west any shadow it casts will move around the opposite way. Use a tall stick if you wish to record the variation in the length of shadows cast by a stick, throughout a day, or at the same time of day throughout a year.

If you want to tell the time from the position of shadows, mark the direction of the shadow on each hour throughout a day, and label it with the times given on a clock. From then on you can tell the time from the position of the stick's shadow.

Sundials work on the same principle as shadow sticks. However, remember that in many countries, including Britain, watches and clocks are put forward in summer (by one hour in our case) to make the evenings lighter. This can save considerable energy consumption for lighting. So during summer, you must add one hour to the 'Sun time' shown on sundials so that they read the same as watches.

Figure 12.7(a) shows a variation of the single shadow-stick. The apparatus is made with polystyrene balls, on vertical wire rods which form a semicircle. You need a rod for each hour of daylight. To find where to put the X on the base, place the apparatus to face due north. On any sunny day, at say 10.00

Figure 12.6

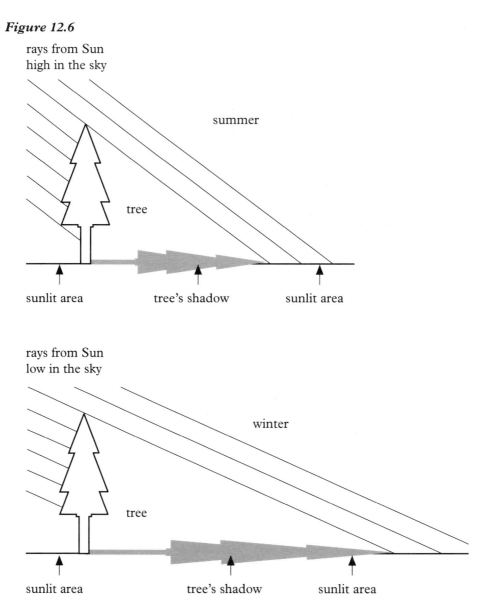

rays from Sun
high in the sky

summer

tree

sunlit area   tree's shadow   sunlit area

rays from Sun
low in the sky

winter

tree

sunlit area   tree's shadow   sunlit area

The lengths of shadows in summer and in winter

hours, draw a line to represent the shadow of the 10.00 hour rod. Repeat that later, say 15.00 hours, using the appropriate rod. Put the X where the two lines cross. The central ball is for midday without adjustment for British Summer Time (13.00 for BST). The others are for use at hourly intervals on either side of midday. On a sunny day, with the apparatus pointing north–south, the balls are adjusted each hour, so that each ball's shadow in

Figure 12.7(a)

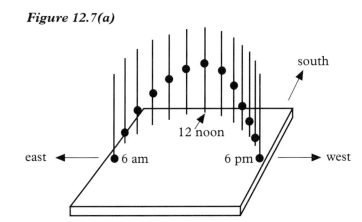

Plotting the path of the Sun across the sky

Figure 12.7(b)

Sun's light

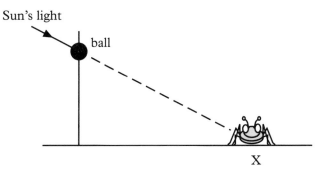

The Sun's light is blocked out by the ball,
forming a shadow of the ball at X.

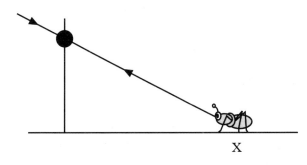

If you were to view the ball from X you
would be looking directly towards the Sun.

Explanation of the apparatus

turn falls on the X. The arc formed by the balls then replicates the Sun's path across the sky. From Figure 12.7(b) you can see why this is so.

For someone looking at our sky, the Sun seems to move across it while the Earth stays still. In fact we can most simply explain the movements we observe of the Sun, other stars and the planets if we imagine the Sun to be 'fixed' and the Earth moving. The Earth spins as though on an axle through its north and south poles. It is because of the Earth's spin that the Sun seems to move across the sky. Deciding whether it is the Earth or the Sun that 'moves' isn't easy. It is rather like sitting in a railway carriage looking at another stationary carriage on the next track. You have probably experienced the odd sensation of thinking your train has started to move off in one direction when in fact it is the other train which is moving the other way while your train is still. Your eyes and brain have fooled you. All you can be sure of is that the two trains have moved relative to one another. Standing on Earth and seeing the Sun move relative to us could mean that the Sun is actually moving around us; or that the Sun is still and we on Earth are moving. There is no easy way of saying which *is* the case. However, it is now generally accepted that the Earth spins on its own axis while the Sun remains 'fixed'.

Figure 12.8 shows Earth as seen from over the North Pole. The Earth, from this view, spins in an anticlockwise direction. A whole Earth day is the time it takes Earth to complete one turn, approximately 24 hours. Notice that 'day-length' does not mean 'hours of daylight'. Britain's positions, as the Earth turns, are shown for midnight, sunrise, midday and sunset. Work around the figure anticlockwise, from (1) to (4). Notice that as the person (supposed to be in Britain) has his or her back to Earth's North Pole, he or she is facing south all the time so will see the Sun in daytime. The best way to understand what is seen is to go into a darkened room and use a lamp for the Sun and your own head for the person on Earth.

Earth's tilt

The explanation of day and night accompanying Figure 12.8 does not account for the variation in the height of the Sun in the sky throughout the year, and to do that we must bring in the tilt of the Earth to the Sun's rays at different times of the year. So now we have to look 'sideways on' at the Earth and the Sun.

In Figure 12.9, we see that looking down on the North Pole, the Earth not

Figure 12.8

The Sun is a long way off in direction

Start here and work anticlockwise

(1) *Midnight*
The Earth's bulk blocks out the sunlight, and it is Britain's night-time

(2) *Sunrise*
As the Earth spins, Britain reaches the position where someone with their back to the North Pole would have to look left to see any sunlight. They would see the Sun rising in the east

(3) *Midday*
As the Earth continues to spin around, the observer has to look straight ahead to see the Sun. He or she is looking south

(4) *Sunset*
The observer has to look to the right to see the Sun, now about to disappear over the horizon

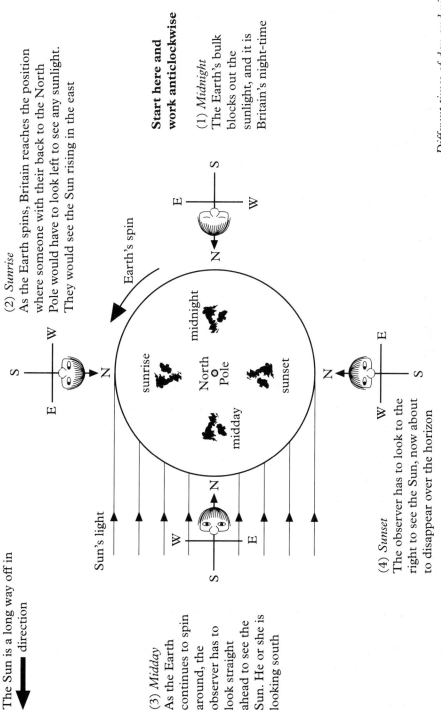

Sun's light

Earth's spin

midnight

sunrise

North Pole

sunset

midday

Different times of day and night

Figure 12.9

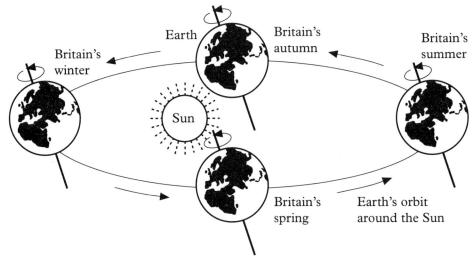

Side view of the tilted Earth in different positions as it orbits the Sun

only spins anticlockwise (once a day), but also orbits the Sun in an anti-clockwise direction. The time it takes the Earth to complete one orbit around the Sun is called one year (one Earth year). The actual tilt of the Earth stays more or less the same throughout the year. During the summer in Britain (i.e. in the northern hemisphere), the Earth is tilted towards the Sun: in winter it is tilted away from the Sun. This has a number of outcomes.

THE APPARENT PATH OF THE SUN (2)

In Figure 12.10 the Earth is shown in two extreme positions in its orbit around the Sun, for summer and for winter in Britain. The reason the Sun seems to trace a curve higher in the sky in summer than in winter depends on the angles between the horizon and the Sun's rays. In each position, the horizon, for someone in Britain, is drawn at a tangent to the Earth. (The overhead direction is at right angles to that. From looking at the distant horizon you have to tilt your eyes up through 90° to see 'overhead'.) In sum-mer, at midday, an observer in Britain, looking first at the horizon, has to raise his or her eyes a long way before looking straight at the Sun (which shouldn't actually be done). Now compare the two parts of Figure 12.10. The Earth has travelled half-way round its orbit of the Sun, keeping its tilt the same. You can see that in winter the angle between the horizon and the Sun's

Figure 12.10

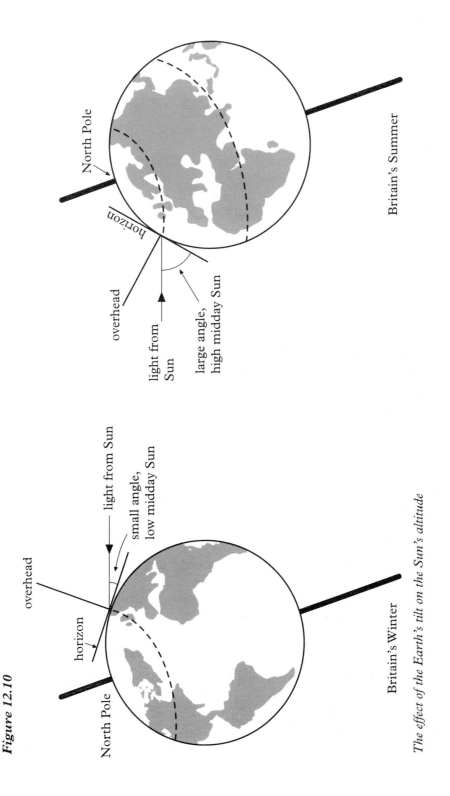

North Pole

overhead

horizon

light from Sun

small angle,
low midday Sun

Britain's Winter

North Pole

overhead

horizon

light from
Sun

large angle,
high midday Sun

Britain's Summer

The effect of the Earth's tilt on the Sun's altitude

rays is small – you need to look fairly low in the sky for the winter Sun, even at midday. A low Sun throughout the day in winter compared to summer means that, at any given time of day, winter shadows are longer than summer ones (see Figure 12.6). In spring and in autumn, the Sun's altitude at a particular time of day (in Britain) is intermediate between those of winter and of summer.

PHASES OF THE MOON

This section has been included because, although pupils are expected to learn that the Moon is spherical, it seldom seems so, and an explanation may be required.

The Moon looks the same shape throughout the time it is visible during any one day. But having observed that the Moon seems to change its shape from day to day, pupils are likely to come up with their own ideas to explain how this happens. These ideas could include clouds or even the Sun obscuring part of the Moon, or a planet's shadow cast on the Moon. The Earth's shadow falling on the Moon, one possible suggestion, does happen occasionally, but only when the Sun, Earth and Moon are in line. This is what causes the eclipse (partial or total) of the Moon, but not the daily changes observed.

The Sun's rays always fall on that half of the Moon which faces the Sun. The Moon completes its orbit of the Earth in about one month, and throughout that time the Moon's shape seems to us to change. This is because we can see only that part of an object (the Moon) from which light is reflected to our eyes. Different parts of the Moon are invisible throughout a month, causing the apparently changing 'shape', i.e. the phases of the Moon.

Figure 12.11(a) shows the Earth and Moon viewed from above the North Pole. An observer in Britain is looking at the Moon's shape at weekly intervals. Figure 12.11(b) shows the observer's views of the Moon. It looks from the two-dimensional diagram as though the Earth should block the Sun's rays, preventing light from reaching the Moon when it is on the far side from the Sun. But in practice this doesn't happen (except in an eclipse of the Moon) because the Moon is not usually quite in line with the Sun and the Earth.

In position A, the observer is on the unlit side of the Earth, so it is night-time for him or her. The Moon's disc is fully lit. The observer sees a fully circular shape, a Full Moon, throughout the night, as shown in Figure

Figure 12.11

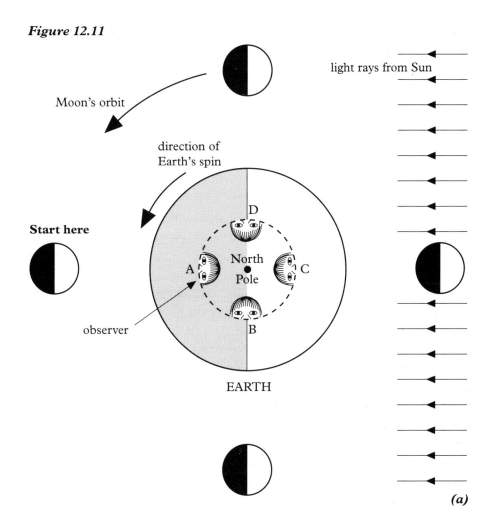

Moon's orbit

direction of
Earth's spin

Start here

North
Pole

A

C

D

B

observer

EARTH

light rays from Sun

(a)

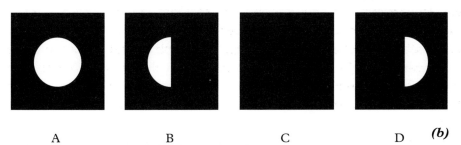

A   B   C   D   *(b)*

Phases of the Moon
(a) The four phases
(b) Observer's view of the four phases

12.11(b). It passes from left to right throughout the night, i.e. from east to west (like the Sun during the day).

If the Moon stayed directly in line with the Earth and Sun while the Earth spins on its own axle and progresses around the Sun, the observer would see exactly the same shape of the Moon (circular) the following night. Also it would be in the same place at the same time as the previous night.

However, the Moon is slowly orbiting the Earth, also anticlockwise. The Moon takes nearly 29½ days to complete one orbit. At the same time on the second night, it will have moved on in its orbit and so will be further east. Its illuminated surface won't quite face the observer. A segment of the Moon on the observer's right-hand side will not be visible. The Moon is waning. It will rise later and remain a little behind in its path compared to the previous night.

One week after Full Moon, the Moon will have moved a quarter of its way round the Earth to B. One half of the Moon's surface is still illuminated, but it is now viewed from a different position on Earth. Only the left-hand half of the Moon is visible. During the days of that week, the Moon's visible shape will have changed gradually from Full Moon to Half Moon (position B in Figure 12.11(b)). As the month goes by, the Moon continues to wane – less and less of it is visible. When the Moon is in position C, between the Sun and the Earth, only the side furthest from Earth is illuminated. The unlit side which faces Earth is not visible – we can hardly see the 'New Moon'. Besides, we are looking into the glare of the Sun. From that time on, the illuminated side (seen from Britain on the right hand) gets larger day by day until, in position D, a half of the Moon's disc is seen. The Moon is waxing. The illuminated area continues to grow until the full disc is again seen, in position A, 29½ days from the first observation. The complete monthly cycle of the Moon is shown in Figure 12.12.

When demonstrating the phases of the Moon, a chair, with the observer sitting on it, can be used to represent the Earth. Use a slide projector, or bright lamp, to represent the Sun and keep that in a fixed position. To represent the Moon, a ball, illuminated on one side by the slide projector, can be carried in a circle around the observer. The complete monthly cycle of the Moon is shown in Figure 12.12, starting, as is usual, with New Moon. The phases A–D correspond to those same labels in Figure 12.11(b).

Figure 12.12

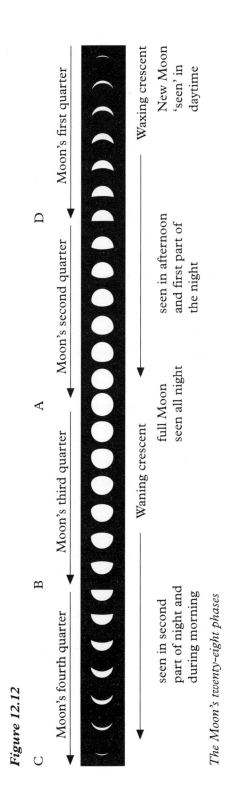

The Moon's twenty-eight phases

SUMMARY

- *Do not look directly at the Sun.*
- Shadows cast on the ground by the Sun indicate its position in the sky.
- The Sun is a huge spherical star, emitting its own light and heat.
- We consider that the Sun is stationary in Space.
- The Moon is a rocky sphere, with no water and no atmosphere, and is smaller than the Earth.
- The Moon emits no light or heat of its own: we see it by sunlight reflected from it.
- We can see only that part of the Moon's surface lit up by the Sun: we see different 'phases' of the Moon.
- The Moon seems to us on Earth to be about the same size as the Sun. This is because although the Sun is much larger, it is much further away in Space than the Moon is.
- The Sun, Moon and Earth all lie roughly in a plane in space, so that the Sun and Moon seem to travel in similar paths around the Earth.
- The Earth's tilt to that plane accounts for seasonal variations, including the apparent changes in the height of the Sun.
- The Earth-day (24 hours) is defined as the time it takes the Earth to complete one revolution on its own axis.
- The Moon takes approximately one day to orbit the Earth, and one month (approximately 28 days) to complete the cycle of the phases of the Moon (from one New Moon to the next).
- One Earth-year is the time it takes the Earth to orbit the Sun, about 364 days.

GLOSSARY

Chapter	Term
3	**Absorption** the way in which substances enter living cells.
5	**Adaptation** change to suit the prevailing conditions.
2	**Adolescence** the period of a person's life immediately before becoming adult.
11	**Air column (sound reproduction)** any tube such as a flute or organ pipe used to produce musical sounds.
9	**Air resistance** see **Resistance (air)**.
2	**Alcohol** any one of a particular group of chemical compounds but commonly used to mean ethyl alcohol which is a product of fermentation of sugar by yeast.
4	**Alga** one of a group of simple green organisms consisting of only one cell, or of many cells, but almost always found in water, e.g. seaweed.
2	**Alimentary canal** the tube leading from mouth to anus through which the food we eat passes.
2	**Alveolus** one of many thin-walled sacs in our lungs within which the transfer of oxygen and carbon dioxide to and from the bloodstream occurs.
6	**Alloy** a metal blended with another metallic (or sometimes non-metallic) substance, e.g. Brass is an alloy which is a mixture of copper and zinc.
8	**Ampère** – (or amp) is the unit of electric current.
4	**Amphibian** one of a group of cold-blooded four-legged animals with backbones, adapted to live both on land and in water, e.g. frog.
11	**Amplitude** a measure of how widely a wave is vibrating. The greater the amplitude of a sound wave the louder it will be.
4	**Animal kingdom** the name given to the group of many-celled animals.
3	**Annual plant** a plant which completes its life cycle within one year, i.e. it germinates, grows, reproduces and dies within this period.
3	**Anther** the part of the plant in which pollen is produced.
4	**Arachnid** one of a group of animals including spiders and scorpions.

2   **Artery** any thick-walled blood vessel carrying blood from the heart to other organs and tissues.

4   **Arthropod** one of a group of animals with jointed limbs and a hard outer skeleton, e.g. insects.

1   **Asexual reproduction** reproduction which does not involve the fusion of two sex cells or gametes.

6   **Atom** the building block of all matter. An atom is the smallest part of an element which can take part in a chemical reaction.

2   **Atrium** either of the two upper chambers of the heart.

2   **Backbone** *see* **Vertebral column**.

5   **Bacterium** any one of a group of simple single-celled living organisms with a cell wall but lacking a true nucleus.

2   **Balanced diet** a diet in which all nutrients are eaten in the recommended proportions.

2   **Balanced forces** *see* **Forces, balanced**.

8   **Battery** Strictly, a battery is made up of two or more electrical cells joined end to end. *See* **Cell**.

3   **Biennial plant** a plant which completes its life cycle in two years. It germinates and grows in the first year, and flowers and sets seed in the second, e.g. foxglove.

6   **Bio-degradability** the ability of some substances to rot away slowly when exposed to air, water and sunshine.

5   **Biosphere** that part of our planet and its surrounding atmosphere which supports life.

4   **Bird** an animal covered with feathers and having scaly legs. Most birds fly.

2   **Blood vessel** a tube which carries blood around our bodies.

2   **Brain** the part of the central nervous system inside our skull where information is received and responses are co-ordinated.

2   **Breathing** the movement of air in and out of our lungs.

10 **Brightness – a) of a light source** The brightness of a bulb or other light source is a measure of how much light energy is emitted each second.
    Brightness – b) of a surface The brightness of a non-luminous surface is a measure of how much light energy it reflects each second.

2   **Bronchus** a tube leading from our windpipe into a lung.

6   **Burning** a chemical reaction in which a substance combines with oxygen in the air producing heat and flames.

2   **Canine (animal)** an animal with well-developed canine teeth, e.g. dog.

2   **Canine (tooth)** a tooth used for tearing flesh.

2   **Capillary** the narrowest type of blood vessel found at the ends of arteries and veins in our tissues.

2   **Carbohydrate** a compound containing the elements carbon, hydrogen and oxygen only, e.g. sugar.

5   **Carbon cycle** a sequence by which carbon circulates and is recycled through the natural world.

1   **Carbon dioxide** a gas present in the atmosphere and used by plants in photosynthesis.

2   **Carcinogen** a substance which has been shown to be capable of causing cells to multiply in an uncontrolled way. (Produces cancer).

5   **Carnivore** an animal which eats the flesh of other animals.

3   **Carpel** the female part of a plant consisting of stigma, style and ovary.

4   **Cartilage** a type of connective tissue which acts as a cushion between bones.

1   **Cell (biological)** the simplest unit capable of independent life. It consists essentially of a nucleus and cytoplasm.

8   **Cell (electrical)** a device which can send electric current through a circuit. (It is often called a battery).

2   **Central nervous system** the brain and spinal cord.

8   **Charge (electric)** the property of some objects that causes them to exert electrical forces on one another. *See* **Force (electrostatic)**.

6   **Chemical change** a change in which a new substance is formed which is unlike the original substance. Usually they are irreversible, unlike **physical changes**.

3   **Chlorophyll** a pigment found in green plants.

2   **Cilia** hair-like structures on the surfaces of some cells. They can allow cells to move from place to place or help to remove particles from cell surfaces.

8   **Circuit** A circuit is made when electrical components are joined in a continuous loop.

2   **Circulatory system** the heart and blood vessels which serve to circulate the blood around our bodies.

2   **Cirrhosis** a disease of the liver which can be caused by excessive drinking of alcohol.

4   **Class** a grouping of organisms used in classification.

4   **Cold-blooded animal** one whose temperature is closely related to that of its surroundings.

6   **Combustion** combustion, or **burning**, are terms often misunderstood by children. Combustion is a chemical reaction in which something reacts with oxygen, usually from the air, evolving heat and forming new substances.

5   **Community** a group of organisms living together in a habitat.

5　　**Competition** organisms vying with one another to obtain food, shelter, etc.

6　　**Compound** chemical substance made of two or more elements, e.g. water is a compound made up of the two elements hydrogen and oxygen.

6　　**Condensation** the process of a gas forming a liquid on cooling.

6,8　**Conductor (electric)** a material or an object which has small resistance to the flow of an electric current so that the current passes through it easily. *See* **Resistance (electric)**.

6　　**Conductor (heat)** a material or an object which allows heat to pass through it easily.

3　　**Coniferous plant** one which produces cones in order to reproduce.

5　　**Consumer** an organism which feeds on other organisms.

2　　**Coronary heart disease** disease of the coronary artery which supplies the heart with blood.

4　　**Crustacean** an arthropod with a hard shell. Most live in water, e.g. crabs but some live on land, e.g. woodlice.

7　　**Crystal** a solid substance in which the atoms or molecules have an orderly three-dimensional arrangement.

6　　**Crystalline** this describes solids which form with a regular shape and straight-line edges because of the way in which the particles which form it line up.

8　　**Current (electric)** the flow of electric charge through a conductor. Unit of current is the ampère, shortened to amp.

10　**Darkness** occurs when no light enters our eyes.

12　**Day** for any planet, one day is the time it takes for the planet to rotate once on its own axis.

11　**Decibel** the unit used to measure the loudness of a sound.

5　　**Decomposer** an organism which feeds on dead organic matter.

1　　**Defecation** the passing out of solid waste material from the anus.

2　　**Development** the process a living organism undergoes as it changes from egg or seed to adult.

2　　**Diet** the food eaten.

2　　**Digestive system** the alimentary canal and associated glands concerned with breaking down and absorbing food.

3　　**Dispersal** *see* **Seed dispersal**.

9　　**Displacement (of water)** a term which can be used for either the volume or the weight of water which is made to move to a new position by a partially or wholly submerged object.

6　　**Dissolving** often confused by children with melting. In melting, a single solid substance turns into its liquid form on heating. In dissolving, a substance becomes part of a solution by being added to a liquid: heat may not be necessary.

2   **Drug** a chemical which affects living cells.

12   **Earth** is the name of the planet on which we live.

12   **Earth's tilt** the tilt of the Earth's imaginary axis to the imaginary plane which contains our Sun and its planets.

4   **Echinoderm** one of a group of spiny, marine animals, e.g. starfish.

5   **Ecology** the study of living organisms in their environment.

5   **Ecosystem** a community of organisms interacting with one another and with their environment, e.g. pond life.

1   **Egg cell** a female gamete.

2   **Ejaculation** the forcing of semen from the penis.

5   **Elasticity** ability of a material to be stretched and return again to its original size and shape.

6, 8 **Electrical conductivity** the ability of a substance to let an electric current flow through it.

8   **Electricity** Any phenomenon which can be explained by stationary electrons (static electricity) or moving electrons (current electricity).

8   **Electron** a very tiny particle which has negative charge. When a voltage is applied free electrons can be made to move in a particular direction, causing an electric current.

9   **Electrostatic force** *see* **Force (electrostatic)**.

6   **Elements** these are substances which cannot be broken down into anything simpler by any chemical process. They consist of one type of atom only.

2   **Embryo** a young plant or animal at a very early stage of development.

3   **Embryo plants** seedlings.

1   **Endocrine system** the system of ductless glands which produce hormones in our bodies.

5   **Environment** surroundings.

2   **Enzyme** a biological catalyst.

6   **Evaporation** the process by which a liquid turns into a gas, not necessarily by boiling.

1   **Excretion** the removal of waste products of our metabolism, e.g. carbon dioxide.

2   **Excretory system** kidneys, bladder and tubes connecting these to the outside of our bodies. Urine is made and excreted via this system.

2   **Exercise** the transformation of energy by our muscles.

2   **Exocrine gland** a gland with a duct, e.g. salivary gland.

2   **Fallopian tube (see Oviduct)** tube along which an egg passes from the ovum and in which fertilisation normally occurs.

1   **Faeces** solid waste material ejected from the anus.

2   **Fats** an energy-rich group of nutrients.

1   **Feeding (in animals)** taking in food.

5   **Feeding (in plants)** not an appropriate term, but is sometimes used for absorption of water and minerals from the soil.

4   **Fern** a plant which reproduces by spores and does not produce flowers, e.g. bracken.

2   **Fertilisation (in animals)** the joining together of male and female gametes.

3   **Fertilisation (in plants)** the joining together of male and female gametes.

2   **Fibre** the part of our food which cannot be digested, chiefly cellulose from plant cell walls.

5   **Filter feeder** an animal which filters small organisms from water for food.

6   **Filtration** separating a solid from a liquid by passing through filter paper or a similar material.

4   **Fish** cold-blooded, scaly animals, with backbones, which live in water.

9   **Floating** occurs when the upthrust on a partially or wholly submerged solid object in a liquid is equal to the weight of the object, the object floats.

3   **Flower** the organ of a flowering plant concerned with reproduction.

3   **Flowering plant** a plant which produces flowers.

2   **Foetus** the name given to a mammalian embryo when it has developed recognisable features.
The human embryo is called a foetus after about 8 weeks.

5   **Food chain** a sequence representing the feeding relationships of plants and animals in a community.

2   **Food classes** groups of foods which are rich in a particular nutrient, e.g. rich in protein.

9   **Force** a push or a pull. A force or forces are needed to change the movement and/or the shape of an object. The unit of force is the newton.

9   **Force (electrostatic)** An electrostatic force exists between two electric charges. Positive charges repel one another, as do negative charges: but a positive and a negative charge attract one another. Unit, newton.

9   **Force (magnetic)** Magnetic forces can be either attractive (between a north and a south pole), or repulsive (between positive charges, or

between negative charges). Magnetic forces also exist between a magnet and 'magnetic materials' (e.g. iron). Unit, newton.

9   **Forcemeter (or spring balance)** is an instrument for measuring the size of a force. It should be marked in newtons.

9   **Forces (balanced)** Two forces which act through the same point of an object are 'balanced' if they are the same size but act in exactly opposite directions.

9   **Forces (unbalanced)** When two forces of different sizes act in opposite directions on an object, the resultant force is 'unbalanced'.

7   **Fossil fuel** coal, oil and natural gas, which are formed from the fossilized remains of plants.

11   **Frequency** the number of sound waves produced in a second. The greater the frequency the higher the pitch of the note.

9   **Friction** the retarding force which acts between two surfaces rubbing together. The brakes on a bicycle or car slow it down because of the forces acting between the brake pads and the wheels. Unit, newton.

3   **Fruit formation** the further development of reproductive structures in plants after fertilisation.

4   **Fungus** a simple organism without chlorophyll which usually feeds on dead organic matter, e.g. yeast.

1   **Gamete** a sex cell.

6   **Gas** a substance above its boiling point, in a state where it has no definite shape and fills any volume in which it is placed. (This is therefore a wider meaning than many children use when they think of the commodity supplied by the Gas Board.)

3   **Germination** the production of a root and shoot from a seed.

5   **Gill** an organ in fish and other aquatic animals used for breathing.

2   **Gland** a collection of cells which produce a particular substance such as an enzyme or a hormone.

9   **Gravity** the force which pulls everything and everyone towards the Earth. Unit, newton.

1, 3   **Growth** an irreversible increase in size. Growth in plants continues throughout life.

5   **Habitat** a place where organisms live.

6   **Hardness** a measure of how difficult it is to scratch a substance.

5   **Hardy plant** one not killed by frost.

2   **Hearing** the ability to detect and react to sound.

2   **Heart** the pump for the circulatory system.

6   **Heat conductor** *see* **Conductor (heat)**.

3   **Herbaceous plant** one whose stem is not woody.

5   **Herbivore** an animal feeding on plants.

4   **Homoeothermic animal** *see* **Warm-blooded animal**.

1   **Hormone** the secretion of an endocrine gland, e.g. thyroscine.

2   **Hunger** the desire for food.

2, 7   **Igneous rocks** tend to have interlocking grains giving the rock a crystalline appearance and formed by the solidification of molten rock or magma that originates deep in the Earth.

2   **Incisor** a type of tooth used for biting off chunks of food.

6   **Insoluble** a substance which will not dissolve in a named liquid. A substance (e.g. tar) may be insoluble in one liquid (water) but soluble in another (paraffin).

8   **Insulator (electrical)**- a material or object through which an electric current cannot pass, no matter how large the applied voltage.

6   **Insulator (thermal)** a very poor conductor of heat.

1   **Invertebrate** an animal without a backbone.

4   **Key** an aid to identification of animals or plants.

2   **Kidney** the organ in which urine is made.

9   **Kilogram (kg)** the international unit of mass.

2   **Large intestine** the lower part of the alimentary canal in which water is absorbed from the faeces.

3   **Leaf** the organ of a plant in which photosynthesis take place.

5   **Legume** one of a group of protein-rich plants which can harbour bacteria able to obtain nitrogen from the atmosphere, e.g. pea.

4   **Lichen** an organism consisting of an alga and a fungus living closely together and supporting one another.

10   **Light** a form of energy. Light is part of a continuous spectrum from radio waves, through infra-red and ultra-violet to gamma rays. The small range within that spectrum to which the human eye responds is known as 'light'.

5   **Light intensity** the strength or brightness of sunlight. *See* **Brightness**.

6   **Liquid** a substance which flows but is not a gas, and which has definite volume but no definite shape.

2   **Liver** the largest organ in our bodies, responsible for many different functions.

11   **Loudness** a measure of the audibility of a sound.

11   **Loudspeaker** a device for converting electrical impulses into sounds.

6   **Magnetic behaviour** the ability of a material to be attracted by a magnet.

9   **Magnetic force** *see* **Force (magnetic)**.

8   **Mains electricity** the electricity delivered to homes and factories

through the National Grid. (It differs from the electricity produced by cells [or batteries] in that it is at a much higher voltage, and the direction in which it flows alternates.)

2   **Malnutrition** too much, too little, or the wrong sort of, food.

4   **Mammal** a warm-blooded, hairy animal which produces milk for its young.

9   **Mass (of an object)** a measure of how difficult it is to get the object moving. Mass also indicates how much 'stuff' or material makes up the object. (Mass and weight are often confused). Unit of mass, gram or kilogram.

2   **Medicine** a) the study of health and disease.

     Medicine b) a drug used to treat disease.

6   **Metamorphic rock** rock which, after its original formation, has been altered in structure and composition by pressure, heat, and chemically active fluids. It often has a crystalline appearance.

5   **Microbe** an organism which can only be studied with the aid of a microscope, e.g. bacteria.

5   **Microclimate** the weather in a small area, which will affect the organisms living there.

5   **Micro-organism** synonym of microbe.

3   **Midrib** the central vein of a leaf.

2   **Mineral** an inorganic naturally occurring substance, which may occur as a crystal, depending on how it has been formed.

2   **Molar** a grinding tooth.

6   **Molecule** a cluster of at least two atoms joined together, e.g. a molecule of water consists of two atoms of hydrogen and one of oxygen. Some molecules (e.g. polythene) can have many thousands of atoms. A compound is the smallest part of a **compound** which can take part in a chemical reaction.

4   **Mollusc** one of a group of animals with a fleshy foot and usually also a shell, e.g. snail.

12   **Moon** any natural satellite which orbits a planet. Our Moon is Earth's only natural satellite.

4   **Moss** a simple green plant found in damp places.

5   **Mould** a type of fungus consisting of long strands.

1   **Movement** change of shape or position.

1   **Muscle** a structure which allows movement to occur.

2   **Musculo-skeletal system** the system of bones and muscles (or other structures)which support an animal's shape and enable movement to occur.

4   **Myriapod** arthropod with many legs, e.g. centipede and millipede.

4   **Naming** identifying.

6   **Natural material** any material which is found in nature and is not manufactured.

3   **Nectar** sugary liquid produced by some flowers to attract insects.

2   **Nervous system** the system of sense organs and nerves which enables us to respond to stimuli.

9   **Newton** the newton is the international unit of force.

5   **Nitrate** the form in which nitrogen is usually absorbed by plants.

5   **Nitrogen cycle** a sequence representing the inter-relationship of different forms of nitrogen present on earth.

5   **Nodule** a lump on a plant. Usually on the roots, nodules are often beneficial since they may contain nitrogen fixing bacteria.

11   **Noise control** any measure to reduce unwanted noise.

5   **Non-hardy plant** one killed by frost.

2   **Oesophagus** tube leading from mouth to stomach.

8   **Ohm** the unit of the resistance of an electrical component.

8   **Ohm's Law** tells us that the current through a resistor is proportional to the potential difference across it, provided all other factors (e.g. its temperature) remain the same.

$$\text{current} = \frac{\text{voltage}}{\text{resistance}} \quad \text{or amps} = \frac{\text{volts}}{\text{ohms}}$$

2   **Oils** fats which are liquid at room temperature.

5   **Omnivore** an animal which feeds on plants and animals.

10   **Opaque** an opaque object is one which you cannot see through. It allows no light to pass through it. Instead, light is absorbed or reflected.

2   **Organ** a structure which has a particular function, e.g. kidney, flower.

2   **Organ system** a system such as alimentary canal which contains many different organs.

2   **Ovary** the structure in a plant or animal where female sex cells are produced.

2   **Oviduct** the tube carrying egg cells away from the ovary and in which fertilisation often takes place.

1   **Ovule** a female egg cell in a flowering plant which, after fertilisation, develops into a seed.

2   **Pain** the sensation of physical hurt or discomfort caused by injury, illness, etc.

7   **Pebble** a rock fragment, usually worn by the action of water, which is larger than a granule but smaller than a cobble.

2   **Penis** male copulatory organ of mammals, some reptiles and some invertebrates.

3   **Perennial plant** a plant able to live for more than one year.

2   **Peripheral nervous system** connection between all parts of the body, the brain and spinal cord. *See* **Central nervous system**.

12   **Phases of the Moon** the apparent shapes of the Moon when all or parts of its illuminated hemisphere faces Earth.

1   **Photosynthesis** reaction in which plants make their food from water and carbon dioxide using energy from the Sun.

6   **Physical change** a change to a substance which does not turn it into a different chemical, and which can be reversed, e.g. ice into water. *See* **Chemical change** for the comparison.

3   **Pigment** coloured substance found in plants and animals.

11   **Pitch** in musical terms, how high or low the note is.

4   **Plant kingdom** name given to the group of organisms which produce food by photosynthesis, and have many cells.

4   **Poikilothermic animal** *see* **Cold-blooded animal**.

3   **Pollen** powder-like substance made by flowering plants which contain male sex cells.

3   **Pollination** transfer of pollen from an anther to a stigma before fertilization.

5   **Pooter** piece of equipment used for collecting small invertebrates by sucking them into a small container.

5   **Population** all the members of the same species of organism living in a defined place.

2   **Position sense** the sense which enables us to mark out the position of our body.

8   **Potential difference** applied to a circuit, sometimes referred to as the 'voltage', is the 'push' which sends the current round the circuit. It is measured in volts.

8   **Potentiometer** a device which produces a variable potential difference, i.e. a variable voltage.

5   **Predator** an animal which eats other animals.

2   **Premolar** tooth with a two-pointed crown, suited for crushing and grinding food.

5   **Prey** an animal which is eaten by a predator.

4   **Primate** group of mammals which includes humans, apes and monkeys.

5   **Producer** organism which makes its own food, and forms the first link in a food chain.

2	**Protein** a compound always containing the elements carbon, hydrogen, oxygen and nitrogen, with many important functions in living organisms.
5	**Protozoan** single celled organism which has many of the characteristics of animals.
2	**Puberty** onset of adolescence.
5	**Rainfall** the amount of rainfall, measured by the depth of water fallen.
2	**Rectum** last part of the alimentary canal which stores indigestible food.
6	**Reflection of light** occurs when light bounces off a surface.
1	**Reproduction** production of new individuals. *See* **Sexual reproduction**.
4	**Reptile** group of cold-blooded vertebrates which includes snakes and lizards.
9	**Resistance (air)** air resistance is the force exerted by the air on an object moving through it. This force, like friction between solids, tends to slow down an object as it moves through the air.
8	**Resistance (electrical)** is a measure of how difficult it is to pass electric current through a component. The unit of resistance is the ohm.
8	**Resistor** An electrical component which has a fixed resistance.
1	**Respiration** process in which energy is released from chemicals inside living cells.
2	**Respiratory system** the lungs and associated tubes.
2	**Rest** relaxation from exercise or labour.
8	**Rheostat** is a device with variable resistance.
2, 7	**Rock** any accumulation of minerals, whether consolidated (stuck together) or not, which forms part of the Earth's crust.
3	**Root hair** hairs which grow out of single cells in young roots and increase the surface area of the root.
2	**Roughage** *see* **Fibre**.
6	**Saturated solution** one in which no more of a particular substance can be dissolved.
2	**Scrotum** sac-like structure containing the testes in mammals.
2, 7	**Sedimentary rocks** tend to be grainy in texture and may contain fossils. They are formed from the fragments of other rocks that have been weathered, eroded and then transported, by water, ice or wind, and finally deposited (settled) as sediments in water or dunes.
3	**Seed** reproductive structure of flowering plants.
3	**Seed dispersal** spreading of seeds from place to place by various means.

1	**Sense organ** a part of an organism sensitive to physical changes or stimuli, e.g. ear.
1	**Sensitivity** ability to respond to stimuli.
2	**Sexual intercourse** process during which male gametes are passed into female body.
2	**Sexual maturity** stage of development when sex cells can be produced.
1, 3	**Sexual reproduction** type of reproduction involving joining together of male and female sex cells.
10	**Shadow** A shadow is the dark space into which no light falls, behind a front-lit, opaque object.
8	**Short circuit** When a component with very little resistance (e.g. connecting wire) is connected across the ends of a cell or battery, a short circuit is made.
3	**Side-stem** stem branching from a main stem or trunk.
6	**Sieving** passing a substance through a wire mesh so that the smaller particles can go through but the larger ones are retained.
2	**Sight** ability to see things.
9	**Sinking** When the upthrust on a solid object in a liquid is less than the weight of the object, the object sinks.
1	**Skeleton** that part of the body which supports the organism.
2	**Small intestine** tube between stomach and large intestine.
4	**Soft-bodied animal** invertebrate animal which does not have a hard outer skeleton.
6	**Solid** any substance that is not free to flow like a liquid.
6	**Soluble** something which will dissolve in a particular liquid, usually water.
6	**Solution** a liquid which has something dissolved in it.
6	**Solvent** any liquid in which something can be dissolved.
11	**Sound** any vibration which can be detected by the human ear.
11	**Sound waves** the to and fro motion of air or whatever is carrying sound outwards from its source.
4	**Species** group of organisms which usually look similar to each other or can interbreed to produce fertile offspring.
9	**Speed** a measure of how far something travels in a certain time in miles per hour, or, using units recommended for science, metres per second.
1	**Sperm cell** male sex cell.
2	**Sperm duct** tube through penis in which sperm travel.
2	**Spinal cord** part of the nervous system running from the brain to the end of the vertebral column.

6   **States of matter** the three main states of matter are solid, liquid and gas.

3   **Stem** part of plant which has leaves and flowers on it.

3   **Stigma** part of the flower which receives pollen.

1   **Stimulus** change in the surroundings of an organism which results in a response.

3   **Stoma** small hole in surface of leaf through which gases and water vapour can pass.

2   **Stomach** part of alimentary canal between oesophagus and small intestine.

7   **Stone** the hard, compact, non-metallic material of which rocks are made.

9   **Streamlined** an object is streamlined if its shape is such that the resistance of the air, or other gas or liquid through which it flows, is very low.

11   **Striking (sound production)** hitting an object (e.g. a drum) to produce a sound.

12   **Sun** the nearest star to Earth, around which Earth and the other planets in our solar system rotate.

6   **Suspension** a liquid containing small solid particles of something which will not dissolve, e.g. a suspension would be obtained by shaking powdered chalk with water.

6   **Synthetic material** any substance which has been manufactured rather than occurring in nature.

5   **Temperature** a measure of how hot something is.

2   **Temperature sensitivity** ability to sense temperature.

2   **Testes** male reproductive organ in animals which produces small cells.

6   **Texture** the feel of a substance, e.g. rough, smooth, woolly.

6   **Thermal conductor** a material through which heat can travel easily.

6   **Thermal insulator** a material through which heat cannot travel easily.

11   **Timbre** When an instrument plays a note, that note is made up of a number of different notes, called harmonics, which gives each instrument its particular sound quality or 'timbre'.

2   **Tooth** hard structure found in mouth of vertebrates used for biting and chewing.

5   **Top predator** final animal in a food chain.

2   **Trachea or 'windpipe'** the tube containing air leading to the lungs.

10   **Translucent** a translucent material allows some of the light which falls onto it to pass through, the rest being scattered or absorbed, e.g. baking parchment.

11   **Transmission of sound** the way in which sound travels outwards from its source.

10   **Transparent** a transparent object is one which allows enough light to pass through it for objects on the far side to be seen clearly, e.g. window glass.

3   **Transport in plants** movement of substances inside plants.

11   **Ultrasonic** sound waves with so high a frequency that they cannot be heard by the human ear.

9   **Upthrust** the upward force exerted by water on an object party or wholly submerged in it. The term is used in relation to liquids, and to air (and other gases). Upthrust is measured in newtons.

1   **Urea** a compound which is formed from excess protein in many animals.

2   **Urethra** a tube taking urine from bladder to outside of body.

2   **Urine** a liquid (water, urea, salts) formed in the kidneys and stored in the bladder before discharge from the body.

2   **Uterus** part of female reproductive system in mammals in which embryos develop.

5   **Vaccine** preparation used to stimulate body to produce antibodies to infectious diseases.

2   **Vagina** tube from the uterus to the exterior, found in female mammals.

2   **Valve** something which allows movement through it in one direction only.

4   **Variation** differences between individuals of the same species.

5   **Vegetative reproduction** reproduction in plants that does not involve joining of sex cells.

2   **Vein (in animals)** thin-walled blood vessel that carries blood towards the heart.

3   **Vein (in plants)** part of plant containing cells which carry water and sugar solution.

2   **Ventilation** process by which air is brought to the lungs.

2   **Ventricle** a chamber of the heart.

2   **Vertebral column** flexible column of bones called vertebrae which run from the neck all along the back.

1   **Vertebrate** animal with a vertebral column.

5   **Virus** extremely small particle consisting of a protein surrounding genetic material which can cause diseases in plants and animals.

2   **Vitamin** substance needed in diet in small amounts to prevent certain types of disease.

8   **Volt** the unit of potential difference or electrical 'push'. Its definition is to do with the amount of energy that is carried by the electric charge.

8   **Voltage** *see* **Potential difference**.

4   **Warm-blooded animal** animal that maintains body temperature at a roughly constant level (about 37°C in mammals, 39°C in birds).

6   **Water cycle** circulation of water in the natural situation.

10   **Watt** a unit of power, or total energy emitted per second. For light bulbs, the energy emitted is in the form of both light and (wasted) heat.

6, 9   **Weight** the heaviness of a substance as measured by scales. An object's weight is the force with which gravity pulls the object down. (Weight and mass are frequently confused.)

2   **Windpipe** *see* **Trachea**.

1   **Wire (sound production)** any wire, string or catgut stretched so that when it is struck or played with a bow it produces a musical note.

2   **Womb** *see* **Uterus**.

3   **Woody plant** plant which has wood in it.

12   **Year** for each planet, its year is the time taken for that planet to travel once around the Sun.

5   **Yeast** single-celled fungus.

1   **Zygote** cell formed by the joining together of a male and a female sex cell.